WITHDRAWN

*TWAYNE'S WORLD AUTHORS SERIES*

*A Survey of the World's Literature*

Sylvia E. Bowman, Indiana University

**GENERAL EDITOR**

# AUSTRALIA

Joseph Jones, University of Texas at Austin

**EDITOR**

Eleanor Dark

*TWAS 382*

Eleanor Dark

# ELEANOR DARK

By A. GROVE DAY

*University of Hawaii*

TWAYNE PUBLISHERS

A DIVISION OF G. K. HALL & CO., BOSTON

**Library of Congress Cataloging in Publication Data**

Day, Arthur Grove, 1904-
  Eleanor Dark.

  (Twayne's world authors series ; TWAS 382 :
Australia)
  Bibliography: p. 155 - 63.
  Includes index.
  1. Dark, Eleanor O'Reilly, 1901-  — Crit-
icism and interpretation.
PR9619.3.D38E5        823        75-23369
ISBN 0-8057-6224-8

Dedicated to
DR. AMOS PATTEN LEIB and LOEL
who know what it is like
to make a book.

# Contents

# About the Author

A. Grove Day, Senior Professor of English, Emeritus, at the University of Hawaii, first met Eleanor Dark in 1965 and thereafter began work on the present volume. He completed this research in 1975, during his fifth period of residence in Australia. Dr. Day, who served for five years as chairman of the Department of English at Hawaii, has published more than a score of books dealing with the history and literature of Western America and the Pacific region. In addition to this volume on Eleanor Dark, he is the author of three other titles in Twayne's World Authors Series: *Louis Becke* (1966), *Robert D. FitzGerald* (1974), and, in collaboration with Edgar C. Knowlton, Jr., *V. Blasco Ibáñez* (1972). He has also written *James A. Michener* (1964) for Twayne's United States Authors Series.

# *Preface*

Looking from the pool terrace on the forty-fifth floor of the midtown Sydney hotel, one can see, spreading to all points of the compass, the red-roofed dwellings of some three million people, residents of Australia's oldest and largest city.

Eastward gleams the expanse of the Tasman Sea, a vast arm of the mighty Pacific. To the south lies Botany Bay, site of the first landing by Europeans on the eastern coast of the continent, when Captain James Cook and the crew of the *Endeavour* reached this land in 1770. To the north stretches away the thousand miles of reef-guarded coastline that Cook's lone exploring vessel barely survived. To the west runs the sunset ridge of the Great Dividing Range, which was a barrier to the first settlers of "New South Wales" for more than a quarter of a century. And almost below, at Sydney Cove, one among the many indentations in one of the world's great harbors, can be seen, surrounded by modern skyscrapers, the site of the first colony ever to be set up in the aged continent — with an area as large as the contiguous forty-eight American states — that used to be called Terra Australis Incognita.

Hard it is, surely, to believe that less than two centuries ago, the region in view was not inhabited by a single European. Save for the cries of a few wandering black tribesmen, the shores of the harbor did not resound with the activities of any people. The land was indeed silent, empty, timeless.

The best account in fiction of the perilous founding and settlement of this Port Jackson region is provided by three volumes by Eleanor Dark, foremost historical novelist of her native country.

My main purpose in preparing the present study is to pay tribute to the achievement of this eminent world author who has produced ten novels of distinction — including half a dozen with modern settings and concerned with the psychologies of a varied set of individuals. All the stories take place in Australia, a South Pacific commonwealth that through the years has been claiming a more and more imposing place in world affairs. I believe that this bio-critical volume will serve as a valuable companion to the future readers of those novels and deepen the appreciation due to a pioneer in modernist technique who was also a leader in voicing concerns that are still timely today. This study, however, should not be taken as a substitute for reading the novels themselves, which are much neglected nowadays. Directing attention to the shelf of fine fiction by Mrs. Dark will be my richest reward.

I began reading the novels of Eleanor Dark when *The Timeless Land*, first book of her historical trilogy, was the October Book-of-the-Month Club Selection in the United States in 1941. Since that time I have read and reread her work with increasing enjoyment. In 1965 my wife and I made a pilgrimage to the spacious home of Mrs. Dark and her husband at the resort town of Katoomba in the Blue Mountains west of Sydney, and we were graciously received and informed about their lives. Another visit in 1975 was the high point of our fifth period of residence in Australia. During the intervening decade I made further studies of Mrs. Dark's writings and corresponded with her about many matters. One contribution of the present volume that should not be overlooked is the opening chapter, which gives the most complete biography available of this prominent Australian author, who has always been unduly reticent about details of her private life and labors.

Why should one read the novels of Eleanor Dark today? There are many reasons. First among them, of course, is the year-to-year evocation of the struggling settlement of New South Wales in the "timeless" trilogy covering the years 1788 through 1814. History — based heavily on factual sources — is delightfully mingled with stories of pioneer families, especially that of a wealthy landowner, which is contrasted with that of a convict outlaw. Secondly, one is continually in touch with a narrative mind that bears a sensitive social conscience and is at all times concerned with liberty and justice for all classes — especially black people like the dispossessed aboriginal inhabitants of Port Jackson. Mrs. Dark was also a very early standard-bearer for justice to women, although she was equally concerned about the survival of a strong family system. Again, she is the author of some of the most graphic and moving accounts of life in twentieth-century Australia, and her descriptions of urban and country scenes evoke a panorama of Australia that bring it to life for readers in other lands far from Capricorn. Her concern for history and setting, however, does not overshadow her interest in people, and one can drift for days at a time in the company of her varied cast of characters. Finally, Mrs. Dark was a pioneer in the annals of Australian literature in her use of modernist narrative methods — such as the interior monologue — which at first aroused irritation among readers who had not yet heard of James Joyce, Aldous Huxley, and Virginia Woolf.

My approach in the following pages has been to treat Mrs. Dark's early work, primarily poetry and short stories, and then to discuss the ten novels as the requirements of space permit. Many aspects of a work of fiction can be considered by the critic. I conceive, however, that the main ingredients are four: theme, action, characterization, and setting. A fifth ingredient — style — might be considered the unifying element that reveals in verbal form the combinations of the leading four. Many special contributions, of course, may be found in a work of richness, and it is the duty of the commentator to elicit these. Inclusion of opinions by other reviewers may from time to time reveal further appreciations.

"Theme" I consider to be the main meaning finally discerned in the narrative — the point of the whole effort. Theme is not a conclusion of fact or a moral message, but a comment on life. It may be difficult to paraphrase the thought content of a work, but unless one knows "what the story is about," he will go astray in judging the success of the other qualities. Sometimes the theme of a novel, with its variations, may embody the philosophy of the author.

"Action" comprises the series of happenings narrated. These may be mental or emotional events as well as physical efforts. In the usual novel the characters face struggles which result in crises and significant final events which resolve the conflicts. Conflicts are used to heighten the action. These are clashes of persons, forces, ideas, or emotions and may be of many sorts. Motivated action equals "plot," which may be complex and may surprisingly reveal theme and character in the chosen setting.

"Characterization" is, of course, the presentation of people who have desires that may or may not be fulfilled through the exercise of personal traits. These are revealed by what they think, say, or do, and the reader most easily believes in characters who seem to be impelled by inner compulsions rather than by the need to enact roles convenient for the author.

"Setting" is the area in time and space in which the action of the characters interprets the theme. The total effect is enhanced if the setting is suitable to the other aspects of the work, rather than presented for its own sake as static description. If the author's theme holds good for various times and places, setting need not be important. If, however, it is unusual or if it works upon the motivations of the characters, the setting should be given in greater depth. If setting is an active part of the novel — as it is in Eleanor Dark's trilogy as well as in several of her other books — then the critic might term the novel one of "atmosphere" or "local color."

Quotations from the novels have been given where pertinent. After all, the first and final areas for critical study lie in the words of the author in the work studied.

Most of the book has been written in Sydney, where I could observe many of the sites mentioned in the novels of Eleanor Dark — and I am once more indebted to numerous people of this Australian metropolis for hospitality and aid. The staffs of the Mitchell and Dixson Libraries in Sydney and the National Library in Canberra have assisted, as always, in providing materials for research. In the United States, Dr. Joseph Jones of the University of Texas has been a valuable source of information as well as an able editor. My Selected Bibliography has required untold days of effort to compile, and these printed materials have been drawn upon heavily for my text. I have, however, utilized many unpublished facts. Not the least of these have come from Eleanor Dark herself, who has not only cooperated in my researches but has given me the privilege of freely quoting from all her printed works.

A. GROVE DAY

*University of Hawaii*

# Chronology

1901    Eleanor O'Reilly born August 26 at Burwood, a suburb of Sydney, only daughter of Dowell Philip O'Reilly, writer and teacher, and Eleanor McCulloch.

1910    Father again stood for Legislative Assembly of New South Wales on the Labour ticket but was defeated; later employed by Federal Land Taxation Office.

1914    Mother died August 6.

1915 -  Schooling at "Redlands," Neutral Bay, Sydney.
1919

1917    Father married again, to his first cousin, Marie Miles.

1920 -  Eleanor employed in office of Sydney solicitor; first poem
1921    published, in *Triad*, June 10, 1921.

1922    Married Dr. Eric Payten Dark, February 1.

1923    In January, Darks moved to Katoomba, N.S.W., where they resided thereafter. Eleanor published first short story, "Take Your Choice," in Sydney *Bulletin* on June 7; began writing first novel, *Slow Dawning*, not published for nearly a decade. Dowell O'Reilly died at Leura on November 5.

1929    Only child, Brian Michael Dark, born February 14.

1932    *Slow Dawning* published in London.

1934    *Prelude to Christopher* published in Sydney; awarded gold medal of Australian Literature Society.

1936    *Return to Coolami*, also awarded gold medal of the society.

1937    *Sun Across the Sky*. Dr. and Mrs. Dark toured United States, studying methods of physiotherapy.

1938    *Waterway*.

1941    *The Timeless Land* (Book-of-the-Month Club Selection for October in United States).

1945    *The Little Company*.

1948    *Storm of Time*.

1951 -   Intermittent residence on Queensland farm.
1957

1953    *No Barrier.*

1959    *Lantana Lane.*

1972    Dr. and Mrs. Dark celebrate golden wedding anniversary.

CHAPTER 1

# The Lady of the Mountains

IN the heart of the Blue Mountains, seventy miles west of Sydney, lies the resort town of Katoomba. On its southern edge, a boomerang throw from a lookout from which tourists can view one of the world's great vistas, sits the house in which Eleanor Dark and her husband have lived for more than fifty years.

This spacious home, "Varuna," lies on a slight rise in the middle of a two-acre plot in which eucalyptus and pine trees tower over flower-bordered lawns and native shrubs from the surrounding bushland. Inside, the house is a citadel of civilized living, a warm refuge from the time-consuming demands of city society. Here the invited guest receives the most sincere hospitality in all the tableland region, the Appalachia of Australia. At this home have been written ten volumes of fiction by one of the most outstanding authors in Australian literature.

Eleanor Dark, novelist and chatelaine of this home, offers the visitor tea beside a blazing log fire, for the western wind is sometimes chill on the spreading plateau. Her handsome face has a tinge of sadness in repose, like the faces of most of us who have survived in a battering century; but when the conversation becomes vehement, her dark eyes flash and a lively expression switches on like a lamp. She is most easily aroused by any threat to her privacy, for to her as an artist, solitude and time to think and write are more precious than all the admiration of autograph hunters.

### I   A Failure Who Did Not Fail

Mrs. Dark is reticent with strangers, truly modest about her achievements, and holds misgivings about publicity. She belongs to no literary clubs or circles, and although she does much in a quiet way to advance the arts in her native land, she makes no public appearances and shuns interviews. She has written no autobiography; she knows of no collection of her letters or papers. The Sydney office of her publisher had to send to London to get a photograph of her. When asked why she had printed some of her early work under a pseudonym, she exclaimed:"I wish I had *never* used my own name! Being a well-known writer has brought me many interruptions, and there are only twenty-four hours in a day. 'Miles Franklin' had the best idea; she could write in peace. An author has as much right to privacy as anybody else."

The home of the Darks is lined with books — hundreds of books, including a good sampling of Australiana. The library includes a text on diathermy and a tract on sociological medicine written by Eleanor's husband, Dr. Eric Payten Dark. His wife's volumes hold no special shelf of honor. The walls are hung with colored prints of early Sydney, gifts of a publisher. Upstairs is a portrait of the doctor in his uniform of World War I. Mrs. Dark, asked if any oil portraits of her were in existence, answered: "No; I'm a very bad sitter." Her husband recently, at the age of eighty-five, retired as a school physician in the region. The couple have been devotedly close over a long married life. Eleanor Dark dedicated *Prelude to Christopher* to her husband, and her chief effort in life has not been to write great books but to maintain a charming home for her husband and son.

"My books have been written at intervals snatched from years as a housewife," she says. "Without servants, it is impossible to keep a home going in Australia unless one is busy most of the time." Fortunately, there are compensations. The home is a landmark of loveliness in a town where the slow encroachment of tourism has brought some ugliness. From her kitchen window Mrs. Dark can watch a bowerbird preening himself in his playground, decorated with flowers and odd objects — always blue ones — snatched from neighborhood yards.

In her garden is the detached workroom that Mrs. Dark designed to ensure her privacy while at work in this studio where her novels and stories were written. Pale walls ornamented with landscapes, books, and mementos make it a perfect retreat. "I covet a brass doorknocker," she wrote to a friend when it was built, "but as the one great salient point of the whole thing is that nobody is ever to knock upon pain of death, I think I shall have to do without it."[1]

The Darks built their own tennis court with pick and shovel, at a cost of a shilling and sixpence, and the doctor still plays a good game. The extensive garden requires hours of labor in the open, with the assistance of the doctor's son, a forestry official.

All Mrs. Dark's books, such as the classic historical novel *The Timeless Land,* were written in longhand in the intervals of housewifery. Daughter of a cherished father who was also an author, Mrs. Dark began as a girl to write verse, went on to short stories and journalism, and, after progressing through a half-dozen novels imbued with modern psychology and literary techniques, produced the trilogy that still stands today as the outstanding monument of Australian historical fiction.

By ancestry — her grandparents were of English, Scottish, Irish, and Welsh stock — Eleanor O'Reilly Dark is a perfect representative of the main groups that early settled Australia.

Her maternal grandmother was named Eliza Howell and came from Wales.[2] She married Andrew Hardie McCulloch, whose father was one of the attorneys listed as having been admitted to the bar in New South Wales in 1844. The author's Scottish grandfather, also named Andrew McCulloch, was elected member of the Legislative Assembly, representing Central Cumberland, a Sydney electorate. He died when Eleanor was a small girl, but his brother, P. V. McCulloch, was a Sydney solicitor for many years. Eleanor Dark's mother, Eleanor McCulloch, for whom she was named, was born on November 11, 1870.

The novelist's Irish grandfather, Thomas O'Reilly, was born to a Westmeath family on December 11, 1819, at Douglas in the Isle of Man. He was the son and grandson of army officers. In the middle of the eighteenth century, three O'Reillys in one generation served in the Spanish army; one of them founded a Spanish branch of this military family. Eleanor's grandfather, however, was a man of peace. He went to Australia as a young man and was ordained a clergyman in the Church of England by the Bishop of Newcastle at Morpeth, New South Wales, in 1850. He served as rector of the Church of St. Thomas at the convict colony of Port Macquarie, north of Sydney, from 1854 to 1860. There he married Gordina Clunes Innes, who died in 1860.

The Reverend Thomas O'Reilly then was appointed canon of St. Philip's Church, which stands in Sydney where the southern end of the great bridge now disgorges its traffic day and night around the church where he presided.[3] He remarried in 1863 — this time to Rosa Smith, the novelist's grandmother, belonging to a large English family of partly French descent. Rosa, educated in France, had come to Australia with her brother-in-law, Captain Martindale, later the first Commissioner for Railways in New South Wales. Her sister Julia was the first wife of Charles Badham, for many years Professor of Classics and Logic at Sydney University.

It was probably this Smith grandmother who brought into the family the talent for literature that was to reveal itself in her son Dowell Philip O'Reilly, an Australian author of note who gave his daughter Eleanor what was probably the strongest urge toward her lifelong devotion to a writing career.

Dowell, born at "Greystanes," residence of the canon at St. Philip's, on July 18, 1865, attended nondenominational Sydney Grammar School. When his clergyman father died, the lad and his brother Thomas helped their mother to run "Hayfield," a preparatory school for boys at the town of Parramatta. Before he was twenty, Dowell published a small volume called *Australian Poems*, and in 1888 a larger one, *A Pedlar's Pack*. Disappointed with its reception, he destroyed all he could find of the edition.

Going into politics, Dowell O'Reilly in 1894 was elected a member of the Legislative Assembly for Parramatta and served four years. He is remembered for making the first motion in favor of women's suffrage carried in the Parliament of New South Wales. After losing his seat in the election of 1898 he began an eleven-year service as a master at his *alma mater*, Sydney Grammar School. He continued to write, but was a perfectionist whose standards of self-criticism, both in writing and speaking, were so high that few could attain them. He was generous and tolerant, and gained the affection of his many friends and of the boys at his school. But he was also sensitive and easily frustrated. Shortly before he died he wrote: "I am a failure. I have attempted many things, writing, teaching, politics, drifted along, done just enough to live." The verdict of posterity is different. He wrote some memorable books, and reared three children. His daughter — perhaps inspired in part by her father's aims and even a desire to compensate for the lack of appreciation he had been granted — became one of Australia's leading novelists and the foremost practitioner of historical fiction of the country.

## II  *American Friendliness Still Recalled*

The novelist's parents, Dowell O'Reilly and Eleanor McCulloch, were married at Parramatta in 1895. Their children were Dowell, nicknamed Pat, born at Parramatta on February 2, 1899 (he died in February, 1926); Eleanor, born at the Sydney suburb of Burwood on August 26, 1901, and given a childish nickname she now wishes forgotten; and Brian, born at Turramurra on June 13, 1905. Brian was nicknamed Barnie by his father, but the rest of the family called him Bim.

The children were brought up to enjoy outdoor life and sport. Their father in 1894, just before his marriage, had gone on a still remembered hike through Tasmania in company with J. Le Gay Brereton, Professor of English at Sydney University. Their experiences as they lived off the land and finally turned up, unshaven and weary but still holding a few shillings remaining from the original thirty with which they started, are amusingly narrated in an essay in Brereton's volume, *Knocking Round* (Sydney, 1930).

Eleanor's mother died when the girl was barely in her teens, on August 6, 1914, about the time of the outbreak of World War I. Her father was to marry again under romantic circumstances. As a boy of fourteen he had been taken to England by his father and had met an aunt, Louisa Smith Miles, and her daughter Marie, then a very small girl. Over the years, Dowell had carried on a correspondence with his aunt, which gradually included "Molly." After his wife's death the letters to Molly became warmer and more personal and at last included an offer of marriage, which was accepted. The lady braved the dangers of wartime sea travel from England to Australia, and in 1917 the couple, who had not seen each other since 1879, were married. The husband's correspondence was published as *Dowell O'Reilly from His Letters* (London, 1927), edited by his wife Molly. Young Eleanor got on with her stepmother very well, and in 1938 dedicated the novel *Waterway* to "M. O'R."

The girl grew up in a literary household but was unaware of the prominence of such callers as Sir Lionel Lindsay and Professor Brereton. She listened to adult talk but much preferred to slip out to play or else to slowly devour the family library, which had a good collection of literature in which she could let her active imagination range.

When Eleanor was nine, the household echoed with politics as her father decided to stand once more for the Legislative Assembly of New South Wales on the Labour ticket. This time, however, he was defeated. He obtained a post in the Federal Land Taxation Office and continued writing. His best-known piece of fiction, *Tears and Triumph* (1913), an expanded short story containing conversations that sound like parodies, was hailed in its time as a very advanced contribution to the "philosophy of sex." In 1920 *Five Corners*, a collection of stories which had appeared in the Sydney *Bulletin* and elsewhere, was published. All this fiction and a selection of

O'Reilly's poems were to be collected in one volume a year after his death.[4]

Eleanor attended several Sydney schools and finished at "Redlands" at Neutral Bay, across from downtown Sydney. During the first year after her mother's death she stayed with her Grandmother McCulloch at Mosman, and one day while coming home from school fell in with Christopher Brennan, a teacher of modern languages at Sydney University who is considered by modern critics to be one of Australia's top poets. Brennan, who as a friend of the family had attended the funeral, invited the fourteen-year-old girl into his house and gave her a copy of his *Poems* (Sydney, 1913), in which he wrote an inscription with the date "Easter, 1915." Eleanor Dark's admiration for Brennan is reflected in at least one novel.

Since mathematics was required for university entrance — a subject Eleanor never mastered — she learned typing and Pitman shorthand, and in May, 1920, started to work in a solicitor's office in the city.

As a child who admired her literary father, Eleanor had learned to read at the age of three and had written her first "story" at seven. Except for appearances in school magazines, her first publication was a poem in a monthly, *Triad* (June 10, 1921, p. 27) entitled "My House," signed with the initials of her pseudonym, "P. O'R." In this verse, fairly typical of most of her magazine poems, she did not — unlike the free-verse scribblers of the time — disdain the resources of rhyme. The theme of the poem is feminist; men are allowed to adventure on their own, but women must stay in the home or the heavens will fall. Ironically, not much time would pass before Eleanor O'Reilly would be able to enjoy a home of her own and a career as well. Throughout much of her work, the secure and happy family is held up as an ideal only rivaled by the vision of a woman competing and succeeding on equal terms with men.

Marriage came when she was twenty. Eleanor O'Reilly on February 1, 1922, was wedded to a friend and former student of her father. The groom was Dr. Eric Payten Dark, a quiet-spoken, Australian ex-officer of the Royal Army Medical Corps and a widower with one son, John Oliver Dark. Dr. Dark was awarded the Military Cross for valor in World War I.

Desiring a calmer life than bustling Sydney could offer, the couple moved in January of the following year to Katoomba, where except for a few intervals they have lived ever since. Their first year was saddened by the death of Dowell O'Reilly in the nearby town of

Leura on November 5, 1923. The couple's only child, Brian Michael, was born on February 14, 1929.

At about this time, despite getting settled in her home, Mrs. Dark wrote her first novel, *Slow Dawning*. Most of it was finished in 1923, but it was not published for almost a decade. However, she did sell poems, short stories, and articles, usually printed under the pseudonym of "Patricia O'Rane." Her first story was published in the *Bulletin* for June 7, 1923, and was called "Take Your Choice," by "P. O'R." The story concerns a woman whose husband, who has lost his memory during the war, turns up on the eve of her wedding to another man. Three alternative endings are furnished, depending upon whether the beloved husband announces his return by letter, telegram, or telephone. The first arrives too late and is lost; the second is burned by the carelessness of the new bridegroom, but the marriage is halted midway; the third message by direct voice brings immediate cancellation of the wedding plans. The odds on a happy ending seem to favor Alexander Graham Bell, but the reader is invited to take his choice in this work of ambiguity anticipating "Rashomon."

Other stories appeared, usually with carefully contrived plots that foreshadowed the actions in Mrs. Dark's early novels. One story, "Wind," was quarried in 1926 from the unpublished *Slow Dawning*. Often these pieces reveal the supposed needs of magazine readers rather than the deep needs of Mrs. Dark's art, which usually requires broader scope. Although she wrote other short fiction, and although several chapters of her latest book, *Lantana Lane* (1959), could stand as excellent short stories, Mrs. Dark was to make her solid reputation in the medium of the novel.

Dr. Dark was a pioneer in Australia in the use of advanced methods of physiotherapy, and in 1937 the couple made a tour of American hospitals from San Francisco to New York and Washington. Everywhere they were greeted by colleagues who demonstrated new equipment and methods that Dr. Dark was able to introduce slowly into his home country. The friendliness of the American doctors and technicians is still remembered with appreciation by the Darks.

III   *"To Retire is Not to Flee"*

Eleanor Dark's first novel, written ten years before it appeared in London in 1932, was entitled *Slow Dawning*. She wishes this 'prentice piece to be forgotten, and has not retained a copy. Actually the work, although clearly inferior to her later novels, shows the qualities that presaged the coming of a fine new talent to Australia and the world.

The first novel of the Eleanor Dark canon is *Prelude to Christopher*, issued in Sydney in 1934 by the late P. R. Stephensen, the stormy petrel of publishing both in Australia and England. It has been termed "a complex of love, eugenics, and abnormal psychology," and involves the founding of a utopian island colony. A trend to melodrama is evident, but the psychological analysis is keen and the technique, using stream of consciousness and compression of action by means of time shifts, was quite modern at the time. The book won for Mrs. Dark the annual gold medal of the Australian Literature Society of Melbourne.

*Return to Coolami*, which like all subsequent volumes was published by William Collins of London, appeared in 1936. Here the time scheme is concentrated into two days and the role of chance is pronounced. Again the emphasis is upon mental conflict, this time between a couple who have married without love. This novel likewise was awarded the gold medal of the Literature Society.

*Sun Across the Sky* (1937) compresses the action into a single day and continues the use of violence, psychological focus, and stream-of-consciousness technique. But the clash here is not primarily between lovers but between two men representing opposing sets of values. Attempting more in the way of the "novel of ideas" and social criticism, Mrs. Dark here achieves less in profound characterization.[5]

*Waterway* (1938) is something of a sequel to *Sun Across the Sky*, and continues the concentration on ideas and varied opinions. There is a wide cast of characters, united loosely by the spreading setting of Sydney Harbor and its busy ferries. The action is again tightly packed, into the unity of a single day.

*The Little Company* appeared in 1945 and reflects the confusion of World War II in the thinking of a group of Sydney civilian "intellectuals" whose radical and abortive attitudes were at odds with the determination of most of their countrymen at the time. A recent critical volume terms *The Little Company* "a panorama of the entire intellectual life of Australia during the twentieth century" which "must rank among the first significant novels of ideas produced in this country."[6] The novel was, however, so highly topical that today it seems markedly dated.

Fortunately, Mrs. Dark had previously turned to a less transient scene — nothing less, in fact, than the earliest history of European colonization of the Australian continent. In the trilogy that was coming, starting in 1941 with *The Timeless Land,* her mature technique, stripped of modernistic experiments, was to make her the foremost Australian historical novelist.

*The Timeless Land* deals with the first settlement on the shores of what is now Sydney Cove; the lives of the transported convicts and their guards, thrown together on a terrifying shore on the other side of the world from England; and the bewilderment of the aboriginal owners of the continent now invaded by strange beings who might as well have arrived in a spacecraft.

This first volume of the series won international applause and was followed in 1948 by *Storm of Time,* dealing with the period after the first governorship and culminating in the clash of wills during the administration of William Bligh of *Bounty* fame — Governor Bligh, a man of more than one mutiny, was deposed by enemies in Sydney who circulated such lampoons as "Is there no *CHRISTIAN* in New South Wales to put a stop to the tyranny of the Governor?" The final volume, *No Barrier* (1953), brings the story up to 1815, when the Blue Mountains had finally been crossed and the first road built to link the seaboard with the great plains of the west. With this achievement the first period of Australian settlement came to an end and a new era opened. Fittingly, the stories of most of the main fictional characters of the trilogy also culminate in the third volume.

The trilogy is fiction but is historically accurate. The action includes the main events and personages of the governorships of Phillip, Hunter, King, Bligh, and Macquarie and is based on profound documentary research. In fact, passages drawn from official archives are sometimes quoted at length, and on no important historical points can the reader find Mrs. Dark at fault. Her research was done not only in her own library but among the manuscripts and chronicles of the Mitchell Library, a section of the Library of New South Wales, which is the world's finest repository of documents on the history of Australia and Oceania. Often Mrs. Dark would travel on a rattling early-morning steam train to Sydney, work all day transcribing yellowed, crabbed manuscripts, and return home on a late train to the mountains with buzzing brain and aching fingers. The longhand copying of documents and the writing of the trilogy gave the author a case of bursitis of the elbow which baffled her husband's medical skill and seriously interfered for several years with her tennis stroke.

The historical components of the trilogy, however, never interfere with the story side. The books mainly show the transformation and interlinking of two families — the Mannions, free settlers from Ireland, and the Prentices, representing the convict element — particularly the father of the latter, who escapes from his guards and lives in the bush with the natives that have been driven from their ancient range by encroaching "civilization." As time comes to the timeless land of the aboriginals, the scene expands, the characters multiply, and the events of the action become more lively and complicated. The dignity and power of the earliest scenes, however, and the pathos of the first contacts, embodied best in noble Governor Phillip and the "savage" Bennilong, are never surpassed. The three books, taken together, were hailed by one important reviewer, Sidney Baker, as the foremost candidate for the title of the Great Australian Novel.

The favorite recreation of the Dark family was bush-walking. Traveling on foot, carrying all their possessions on their backs and usually accompanied by their son, they hiked through most of the Blue Mountains and in many other parts of Australia. The wild country described by Mrs. Dark in her novels is as well known to her as the downtown streets of Sydney or the waterways of its harbor. In preparation for writing *The Timeless Land* the Darks followed the forest track of the Dawes group in 1789 in the earliest effort to solve the mystery of the Blue Mountain maze — an effort which, like all the rest for twenty-two years thereafter, ended in a *cul de sac* in the bush. The Darks followed a straight line from Emu Plains to Mount Hay. They camped by the light of blazing gum-tree branches and, wary of poisonous snakes, slept under a sandstone overhang in the unpeopled hills.

Mrs. Dark is the only writer known to possess a secret cave, comparable to that inhabited by Johnny Prentice in *No Barrier*. "We looked for one for years," she once said. "We looked here and we looked there and then one day as we gazed across a gorge from the top of an escarpment we spotted a narrow gash in the cliff opposite, just above a creek." Some years later they made their way to the place. After having a neighbor blast to pieces a large rock, they set about making the cave habitable. "We carried the clay of an old termitarium from up the creek and packed down to make a floor. We divided the cave into two rooms, a lounge room and a bedroom. We built fireplaces, took out some tools and hessian and made chairs and beds. For a table we use a slab of rock. We dammed the creek and made a fine swimming pool, plugging the dam with a removable plug so that we could release the water when we liked. It is a fine place. We go there periodically for relaxation, to forget the horrors of the world for a while."[7]

Eleanor Dark is fond of travel but hates ships and airplanes. Unlike many Australians of her class, she has never been to England but has observed much of her own continent closely. An article, "They All Come Back," appearing in *Walkabout* for January 1, 1951, describing a tour of the "dead heart" of Central Australia, is only one of the writings to result from her travels.

Mrs. Dark has had two secret ambitions. One was to be fulfilled and one was not. According to a close friend writing in 1951: "If you were to ask Eleanor Dark had she, with her literary success, come close to fulfilling her greatest ambition, she would answer without hesitation, 'No, I always wanted to act.' She might add, with a smile, but still quite seriously, 'And I've wanted a place where I could grow three trees together — a jacaranda, a coral tree, and a silky oak — blue, red, and old gold.' Lately she has bought a place on the Blackall Range, a pied-à-terre where it is possible, as it was not in the Blue Mountains, to grow her three trees."[8]

The Queensland adventure began in 1951 when Dr. Dark decided to retire from general practice and spend part of each year "on the land" near their son, who was growing pineapples in a region later well described by Mrs. Dark in a travel article.[9] This picturesque, quiet region lies some seventy miles north of Brisbane, not far from the sea that washes the Great Barrier Reef. Here, forsaking their comfortable Katoomba home for at least six months of each year between 1951 and 1957, the Dark family dwelt among the people — many of them refugees from stifling city life — who struggle to make at least a subsistence living on small homesteads in the Queensland cyclone belt. The Darks raised citrus fruits but specialized in the local macadamia nut which in Hawaii has developed into a million-dollar industry. In its native Queensland the "bopple nut" crop was somewhat neglected, and the Dark family at one time suppled one-ninth of the state's total commercial harvest.

One unexpected by-product of their agricultural activity was Mrs. Dark's latest book, *Lantana Lane* (1959). The characters were fic-tionalized or invented neighbors (except for a one-eyed kookaburra or "laughing jackass" bird named Nelson), but the incidents, if slightly embroidered, were often true. The volume that finally appeared is in surprising contrast with all her earlier writing. Sunny, chatty, full of fun that at times is uproarious, *Lantana Lane* is a book that would bring joy to many thousands were it more widely known.

The silence of Eleanor Dark since 1959 may be interpreted as a result of home duties. Her family now includes seven grandchildren, four belonging to the family of her son Michael and three to that of her stepson John. As one who has made such an outstanding career in Australian literature, Mrs. Dark should certainly be entitled to rest on her laurels, if it happened that she valued greatly the world's laurels. "To retire is not to flee," wrote Cervantes; and admirers of Eleanor Dark's novels around the world are still voicing their admiration for the books that emerged from the house in the Blue Mountains.

# CHAPTER 2

# *Time of Growing*

E LEANOR DARK, child of a literary family, began to appear in print at the age of twenty. Her talent was first expressed in verses, and soon she added the short story to her repertory. Her first novel, most of it written the year after her marriage, was not to be printed, however, until nine years later. A survey of this earlier work is essential to an understanding of her development and later achievement.

The young writer published about a score of poems between 1921 and 1934 (see Bibliography), all of them signed by "P. O'R." The security of a pseudonym presumably enabled her to speak in verse freely and to reveal sentiments echoing a woman's hopes and dreams.

The poem with which she broke into print, entitled "My House,"[1] reveals an early preoccupation with the dilemma of womanhood that is still pertinent in these liberated days: can a woman find masculine freedom and adventure, or must she always remain at home and maintain the species? Through her life Eleanor Dark insisted that the role of wife and mother was the better one.

> Over the road from my house is a wood
> Of tall mysterious trees and shadows dense;
> Of flickering cobweb sunshine and a throng
> Of mysteries for which I look and long —
> But all the world must fail if I go hence.
>
> Over the road from my house in the wood
> Are fancies, wishes, evils, hopes and fears;
> Dark hollows and smooth glades and whispering streams
> But I stand always at my door, with dreams
> Of what I may not know through endless years.

Over the road from my house, in the wood
The men live life; and every woman's son
May seek his man-made gods, may stake his all
On one swift impulse; run — or stand — or fall —
A man's life is his own, and owed to none.

And here behind me all my daughters crowd,
With eager eyes and hands, and whispers tense
With wonder and conjecture, but I press
Them back in spite of mine own restlessness —
"Nay, all the world must fail if we go hence."

The poems are competent and clear, and undoubtedly provided excellent training for Eleanor Dark's prose; but the sharpened dedication of the born poet is lacking. As noted by an interviewer during World War II, "From childhood she had continued to write verses, for which she had a remarkable facility and which, once broken into print, she had no difficulty in selling. If she wanted a few shillings she had only to sit down and toss off some verses. Prose, however, she wrote with 'frightful difficulty.' "

The comment continues: "Eleanor's whole attitude towards her verse was flippant. She states that she knew she was not in the least a poet. She paid no serious attention to a pseudo-talent, a mere facility for rhyming. In later years she ceased to write verse to any extent and not at all for publication. Most prose writers begin as poets, she thinks. Writing poetry seems the natural thing to do when one is young. If there is any real gift the writer develops along that line but if not he switches over onto prose."[2]

## I   A Revelation by Moonlight

Eleanor O'Reilly soon switched to prose. Her short stories, published over more than two decades, reveal a wide range of interests. All show a certain smooth, popular appeal, verging on slickness, that cannot be found in every one of her novels.

After "Take Your Choice" (1923), her first story, mentioned in chapter 1, more than two years passed before the *Bulletin* accepted another.[3] This was "The Book, the Bishop, and the Ban," by "Patricia O'Rane," a farcical treatment of the value of censorship in aiding the sensational novelist. Eustace Neville loves Esmerelda, daughter of the Peanut Brittle King, but his book manuscript is hopelessly Victorian. His fiancée, determined that he shall become rich and famous enough to win her father's consent, rewrites the novel and designs an enticing jacket. She then persuades Monty Muff, nephew of the bishop, to get his uncle to state that for licentiousness and salaciousness he has never seen its equal. The bishop obligingly denounces the work from the pulpit, the book is a best-seller, daddy gives his consent, and the newlyweds are assured of a comfortable life. Suggestive publicity "always works." Neither the theme nor the treatment was very new even in 1925, but censorship has always been grimly rigid in Australia, and hence any mockery of it would appeal strongly to most readers.

"Wheels," another by "Patricia O'Rane," is in many ways the writer's best *Bulletin* story. Mrs. Brand's chief trait is peering into the minds of others and revealing their weaknesses. Her husband, who had no illusions about her, "saw her draw from their souls things long hidden and unknown even to themselves; he saw them wince and shrink, feeling the fear and pain, yet never connecting it with this beautiful, brilliant-eyed young woman who was so sympathetic and listened so patiently." A new victim appears in Miss Wyndham, science teacher in the local school, who had known Mr. Brand some years before. But the victim, whose friend had been hurt by Mrs. Brand's "mental vivisection," is able for the first time to wound the cruel woman with her own weapons, and to expose her childlessness as her inmost shame. Capping Mrs. Brand's admission that she "likes to see the wheels go round," the visitor replies: "You should see my wheels as they go round now — as they have gone round for the last twelve years — ever since your husband was my lover and the father of my little son. . . . I loved him. I lost him and my baby. Ever since I have been lonely. Those are my wheels — there's nothing else."[4] This story reveals Mrs. Dark's continuing interest in marriage, home, and children — and perhaps a guilty feeling that her novelist's intense trait of probing into human minds might become a vice that could bring just punishment.

"Impulse" appeared in the *Bulletin* on January 21, 1931. The melodramatic action is set in the mountains that the author knew so well. Two men meet on a hazardous hillside, and the elder recognizes the younger as the creature who had destroyed his daughter's life. He plans an act of vengeance, but when by accident the villain starts to fall to his death, the injured father on a humane impulse risks his own life to save him. He then, ironically, exacts his vengeance in full. This story is rather masculine in tone, and the O. Henry plot seems mechanical.

"Wind," as mentioned in chapter 1, is a longer story which drew upon the unpublished novel *Slow Dawning*. The names of the two main women characters are identical — Dr. Valerie Spencer and her friend Kitty — but the latter marries "Norman," with whom Valerie had always been in love. The only doctor available when Kitty is dying of pneumonia, Valerie does her best to save her friend, but the venomous tongues of small-town slanderers repeat that she did not try to save Mrs. Bolton, because she wanted to marry her husband. Norman realizes that he cannot be unfaithful to his wife's memory and that another marriage is impossible. Most of the other complications of the novel, such as Kitty's baby, are omitted, and the ending differs as well. In "Wind," Valerie decides to take kindly to Dr. McNab's advice and leave the town, to seek a truer husband and children elsewhere.

Mrs. Dark's next published story, surprisingly, is an early excursion into what had not then been labeled "science fiction." It is humorous and presupposes an invention now classified by the addicts as "teleportation." Called "How Uncle Aubrey Went to London," this *Bulletin* story of 1928 might well appear in one of the anthologies today. It is narrated in the future, when travelers are shipped by radio waves through "Amalgamated Wireless Travels (Human Department)." "It was not," says the niece, "until they realized that they must make a different combination of sense-records for every person that they achieved the perfect smoothness and unity between mind and body that makes the trip a delight now." Uncle Aubrey arrives in London with a leg replaced by one belonging to an irate colonel. Efforts to resolve the mistake result in his exchanging both legs with the other victim. At last, after the delay caused by the London - Paris rush is handled, Uncle Aubrey is assembled properly, but he returns to Australia more slowly by plane. Again the main interest stems from Mrs. Dark's medical background and her speculations about the disparities of mind and body.

The first short story signed by Eleanor Dark in the *Bulletin* came out in the same year as *Prelude to Christopher*. "Hear My Prayer" is especially interesting because of its attitude toward religion and because of its setting around the church in which her grandfather was a canon. Actually the main character, Brian Richard O'Brien, a medical student, is a grandson of a canon similar to the Rev. Thomas O'Reilly, and lives in "Stonycross," a parsonage resembling O'Reilly's "Greystanes" near St. Philip's Church in Sydney. Converted into a boardinghouse run by two pious spinsters, it is the home of the narrator, young Brian, and, later, of his cousin Martin, candidate for divinity. Martin is a practitioner of "canon-worship" and is shocked by the worldliness of Brian's friends and Brian himself, who, goaded by the "never-fading influence of my father's anything but saintly life," tells the story of the innocent canon's most famous *faux pas*. The climax comes when Brian goes one night to Martin's room and, unobserved, sees the young man on his knees, confessing that he is in danger of losing his faith unless God reveals Himself by a sign. Accidentally Brian opens the curtain and a dazzling ray of moonlight falls upon the uplifted face. Thereafter Brian can only speculate how much coincidence and a phase of the moon might have affected the ultimate fame of his cousin Martin, the bishop.

## II  *Explaining the Ways of Love*

"Murder on the Ninth Green," another *Bulletin* story signed by Eleanor Dark, is a lengthy and rather routine attempt to satisfy the demand for mystery yarns and was headlined "a thrilling crime-detection story." Again it is a competent product in a field new to her, but Mrs. Dark thereafter wisely left to a legion of other writers the devising of odd murders and tricky solutions. A doctor appears in the story, but medical life is not of chief interest.

However, in "The Urgent Call," one of the two stories that were published under her own name in the popular women's journal *Home*, Eleanor Dark presents a protagonist who is a doctor's wife. The focus is upon this woman's mind in crisis. She has been painfully ill, but her husband is summoned in the middle of the night by telephone, that fiendish instrument to which a country medico is enslaved. Now, aged sixty and childless, the woman comprehends dully that she, too, has been enslaved — to a spotless home. After thirty-five years, she and her husband are "intimate strangers." He has told her, "You're just a Martha," and as she wanders in pain and darkness through the home she has created, she realizes "that all her life had gone by in the pursuit of something so utterly unsatisfying as a lovely house." She feels a seizure and struggles to the telephone, but her "urgent call" fails to get through and the reader understands that she goes to her end without the ministrations of her doctor/husband. One should not seek autobiography in such a minor bit of writing, but again the wife of a country doctor is portrayed, and perhaps there is also an echo of the feeling that merely to have a husband and to serve as a skilled housekeeper is not enough of a career for a woman of ability.

"Publicity," the other item published in *Home*, is little more than a sketch. A woman convalescing in a hospital hears over the radio the homely recollections of an aged pioneer mother. These touching and honest reminiscences are crudely warped by the announcer into a commercial blurb for rheumatism pills, but humanity prevails even over the air when the old lady has the last words: "Good night, dears."

A short story, "The Curtain," appeared in the first (and last) issue of *Australian Mercury*, edited by P. R. Stephensen. An aging theatrical producer, to whom "nothing dramatic" had ever happened, fails as director of an amateur troupe. He is unable to support his invalid wife, and plans an "accidental" death to obtain insurance for her. He stands on a cliff at sunset and has "a dim, momentary conception of the Deity as a fellow producer — a bit of a bungler, really. Splendid stage — splendid setting — what was He about, anyhow, to spoil a man's exit like this — ?"

The final piece of published short fiction by Mrs. Dark came in postwar 1946, almost a quarter of a century after her first venture. "Water in Moko Creek" likewise has little plot. Four bush-walkers come unexpectedly upon a shady pool among the mountains and take an hour's rest. One of them is a woman who knows that, "while your heart has the power to aid and abet you, you will force your body to seek its hardships now and then. . . . Something has brought you here, and it is no outer compulsion. That is the only thing which seems to be important, and now, in these dreadful days of bullied and coerced humanity, much more important than it ever was before."[5] Henry, the practical-minded hiker, wants to push on quickly to keep to schedule, but the others make him delay while they boil a billy for a leisurely tea. The theme seems to be that the precious water and fire which bring comfort may often be misused by mankind, but that there is a deep instinct which keeps them remembered and renewed through effort. It was also, perhaps, a farewell to the days when the author's slight frame could keep up with the menfolk on the ascent of a steep trail. "For there must come a time when one can no longer put a twenty-five-pound pack on one's shoulders and cover anything up to thirty miles of rough, mountain country — and surely that time was perilously close?"[6]

This survey of Eleanor Dark's short fiction reveals that few generalizations can be made about it. Every short story is of a slightly different type than the others. All show a craftsmanship necessary in magazine writing and some have the slickness of pot-boilers. On the other hand, the best examples have a touch of her own life and, in their way, are more revealing than the "Patricia O'Rane" poems. Yet one can conclude that neither the short stories nor the poems form the medium in which this writer was most comfortable. Her greatest art required the broad canvas of the novel.

As has been said, Mrs. Dark began her first novel in 1923, a year after her marriage and the same year that saw her first short story in print. She and her husband had moved to Katoomba and, while publishing shorter fiction, she found time to write most of *Slow Dawning*. It is about a woman doctor, a character depicted at a time when such heroines were fewer than nowadays and the medical profession had not been so overworked in popular literature.

The book did not find a publisher until 1932, when it was brought out by John Lane in London.[7] It presumably satisfied the readership of that firm, and for a first novel held some good qualities and promise of better to come. An examination of its appealing traits will serve as a basis for appreciation of later accomplishment in the novel form.

The action of *Slow Dawning* is well calculated to maintain suspense. A quotation from the Oath of Hippocrates forms an epigraph for the book, and the main character is a woman medico in a small town three hours by car from Sydney. Valerie Spencer had grown up in Kawarra, where Jim Hunter had been her comrade. When he went off to World War I, he realized that Valerie was "a woman with wide horizons, with strange knowledge of Life and its two gates, Birth and Death. . . . For the first time he felt a faint hostility — not for her, but for her brains" (19).[8]

Brilliant and beautiful, Valerie, a newly fledged M.D. at twenty-five who has lost her parents, returns to her hometown to start a practice, under the kindly guidance of McNab, the only other doctor in Kawarra. She is invited to an engagement party for her best friend, Kitty Ray. A shock comes when she is introduced to the prospective groom. It is Jim Hunter, successful businessman and owner of the local sawmill, who returned from the War seeking nothing but peace — almost to the point of stagnation. And to him, Valerie had symbolized striving.

Valerie realizes that she has always loved Jim but is able to keep her composure, because she suffers her panics in advance. "No one knew of the hours alone before these events, when her soul, like the ridiculous but strangely pathetic White Queen, went screaming through the woods of hysteria" (39). And Jim, in his turn, realizes that he has always loved Valerie. "But it had taken only one glimpse of her at Dr. McNab's, all shining, silvery grey, erect and beautiful, looking, as Morton Leigh had said, 'like a sword,' to startle him to the very depths of his soul" (62).

The planned marriage must go ahead, and Valerie, since Kitty's mother never told her any of the facts of life, has to suffer the torture of explaining them to her innocent friend. "Not only must she lose Jim, but she must sit here and explain to this undeveloped child, who was to be his bride, the ways of love, the origin of the children that would be his" (65).

After the wedding, Jim finds that Kitty rouses in him everything but love. For her part, Valerie when facing Jim feels love, stark and uncontrolled. But she conceals it and through loyalty to Kitty refrains from stealing her husband.

### III   *Hippocrates in the Blue Mountains*

Dr. Gerald Hughes, an attractive but caddish young physician in the next town, pays much attention to Valerie and consults her on several cases. The full realization of what Jim has lost does not come to him until he sees this other man maneuvering to carry off the prize. But Kitty is about to have a baby.

Kitty insists that Valerie attend the birth — a further turn of the torture screw. Valerie does her best, but the baby is stillborn. Kitty's mother, who is jealous of Valerie's influence over her daughter, hysterically accuses the lady doctor of murdering the child, and the evil tongues of country-town gossip begin to wag, recalling the youthful romance between Valerie and Jim.

Book Two introduces Dr. Owen Heriot, a dark-haired, dark-eyed man in his late thirties, six feet tall and with shoulders to match. He has survived four years of war and two years of recovering from a bad wound, and now is determined to push ahead and interlope in Kawarra. Dr. McNab is getting old, and as for the woman doctor — she will have to take her chances as an intruder in a man's profession. Heriot's face, though well featured, "was not a face one cared to watch; one felt that he was sneering at the world in general, which was bad, and that he included himself in the sneer, which was worse" (136). He rents a cottage across the road from Valerie's and competes for patients.

Jim, "a very primitive person," feels like an exile. When his car breaks down and he is picked up by Valerie, he tries to win her, but is rejected, even though her love is still strong.

Dr. Hughes is seen coming out of Valerie's house at three in the morning, after she had served as his anesthetist at an operation.

Heriot realizes that he himself has fallen in love with Valerie. He uses his wound as an excuse to consult her, and finds that she is tired and discouraged, and the victim of anonymous letters inspired by Jim Hunter's pathological mother-in-law.

Valerie still loves Jim and fends off the gruff but sympathetic Heriot. When Heriot's wound becomes worse, she sucessfully operates.

A climax comes when, during Dr. McNab's holiday and Heriot's hospitalization, a hurricane hits the region and Valerie is the only doctor available to attend sufferers in the district. Heriot tells her that, since she loves Jim but also loves Kitty, she is attempting an impossible task if she remains in Kawarra, but is answered: "I won't run away."

Exhausted by driving through the storm and working for thirty-six hours at a stretch, Valerie is summoned to the Hunter home. Kitty is in the last stages of pneumonia. Her efforts fail once more, and she has to face Mrs. Ray's accusation: "You killed her! . . . You could have saved her, only you want Jim for yourself!" (248). But Jim loves his wife for the first time, now that she is gone. As Valerie, who knows Jim so well, puts it to herself: "And because he was faithless in his thoughts to Kitty while she was alive, he thinks he can atone now by being faithful when she is dead" (256). Both Valerie and Jim are legally free, but barred by his emotions. And she is still the target of what Dr. McNab calls "credulity, the love o' sensation, the love o' scandal, and prudery — prudery" (260).

Heriot, against his own interest, suggests to Jim that he see Val. Jim proposes, but Valerie says: "Kitty and I have changed places. Is that it?" and turns down his offer. She now has rejected three suitors, for Hughes and Heriot have also proposed.

A culmination comes when Heriot and Valerie argue her aims, and she offers a strong feminist plea: some women should be free to use both their brains and sex, to have careers and the satisfactions of womanhood as well. Heriot offers himself: "I'm thirty-eight to your twenty-seven, and a bit of a crock into the bargain." She accepts his offer of a trial companionship, spending a few days in a cottage in a valley of the Blue Mountains. Valerie, on the final page, states the final turn of theme. Romance is something of a girlish dream. Her love for Jim has been the attraction of opposites — he was so "normal," and she was exceptional. She marries Heriot, and Kawarra's medical needs will be taken care of by a professional couple devoted to each other and to Hippocrates.

A shallowness of characterization is the chief weakness of *Slow*

*Dawning.* Most of the figures are drawn from the stock shelf. From the start, Valerie is too perfect for belief. "She was always top in her class. Before she left she was also leader of all the games, and on every committee in the school. Her determination to be a doctor never wavered" (14). As a heroine she has no flaw, no feminine frailty that would endear her to the reader and to the three men who battle for her hand. At worst, when torn by fatigue and victimized by gossip, she responds only with a saintly, controlled self-sacrifice. None of the other characters is especially lifelike except, perhaps, the evil mother-in-law, Mrs. Ray.

The style of *Slow Dawning* is not immature; technique must have come to Eleanor Dark early, perhaps because of her family background and early reading. "The command of technique she seems to have possessed from the outset. Whatever the shortcomings of *Slow Dawning,* it has none of the formal ineptitude of the first novel, and displays something of the intensity that is born of severe compression."[9] "The work is immature; but the same ability to handle words is there, and the earliest expression — tentative and uncertain, perhaps — of that extraordinary power to 'open up' and display a mind, that was to make her later books remarkable."[10] H. M. Green's considered judgment is that it is "fresh, sincere, interesting, and intensely alive."[11]

The best aspect of this novel is the setting. One does get a feeling of what it might be like to practice medicine in an Australian country town. Details of cases, drawn from observation of her husband and his colleagues, sound authentic, and although Sinclair Lewis, as early as 1921 in *Main Street,* had debunked the glamor of the life of a small-town doctor, *Slow Dawning* when written still had the air of discovery. Conversations ring truer when a medico is dickering with his Sydney agent than when Valerie is declaiming on women's rights or the duties of lovers and wives. The psychology of a woman was to be more searingly exposed in Eleanor Dark's second novel, *Prelude to Christopher.*

## CHAPTER 3

# Time of Madness and Method

ELEANOR DARK'S first acknowledged novel, *Prelude to Christopher* (1934), reveals a deep interest in abnormal psychology and human heredity. The suffering of a distressed mind — that of the wife, Linda — gradually overpowers interest in the behavior of the ordinary people in the story.

As one critic noted, the book is scarcely a prelude, but rather the fifth act of a tragedy. The outcome, however, is a prologue to the life of a child that eventually will be born to a couple uniting after a stormy crisis.

The theme of *Prelude to Christopher* reveals a conviction that the strongest drives in human biology may be twisted by hereditary defects, which sooner or later will bring the collapse of normal dreams of happiness. Midway in the book, Linda, with her biological training, proclaims to herself: "The two most powerful urges of humanity — self-preservation and the reproduction of one's kind. Heaven help poor Linda, driven by the ancestral instincts of uncountable millions in a million generations!" (104).[1] And "Life," the maimed husband Nigel concludes, "was a manure heap, where the fine flowers of human behavior, the courage, the humor, the endurance, sprang gorgeously to a wild and over-stimulated magnificence. Forced and goaded, they bloomed gloriously and died, and fell back into the filth that had fed them. What mightn't they have achieved, he wondered, growing thickly and sturdily in a good soil, flowering long, fading slowly, dropping their seed into the fruitful earth" (178).

The conflict within Linda, therefore, sways between survival and the drive of motherhood. This simple contrast implies, however, a broad philosophy of twentieth-century naturalism, a pessimistic determinism that was shared in the 1930s by many other serious novelists around the world. The idea that life is a trap for suffering human beings is reinforced throughout the book, and the growing insanity of Linda overshadows the reader's concern for the other persons in the story, who are revealed, as she is, through their reveries.

The action of this book is compressed into four days. Part One, "Tuesday," literally opens with a bang. Nigel Hendon, a forty-six-year-old country doctor driving home to Moondoona, is injured when his car is hit by a van. During his suffering in the cottage hospital, he recalls, in various flashbacks, his early life. Especially does he remember his meeting one afternoon with an old sailor, who told him of a paradisiacal South Sea island, and a meeting that evening with Linda Hamlin, who was to become his wife of the next twenty-three years.

Linda is a strange person who has been conditioned by living with her uncle, a medical biologist with a tainted pedigree. Sadistically, he impresses upon his niece the possibility that the family madness might become dominant in her. Nigel had yearned to exercise his strong vitality toward some high goal, some "magnificent fulfillment," and apparently was to spend five years building an ideal community on the island he finds; but previously, impelled by a conventional, religious mother, he marries Linda and now has settled for a country existence with her that makes him feel that his death might settle all his problems.

Linda visits the sleeping Nigel in the hospital, and silently recalls their first meeting in Sydney years earlier. Her dark beauty, at the age of forty, contrasts with the blond wholesomeness of Kay Mannering, the twenty-two-year-old nurse who comes to the bedside. As Nigel begins to revive, Linda leaves with a sarcastic remark, and Kay comforts the patient in his sickness.

Back in her home, Linda stares at her image in the mirror and feels that her evil uncle has transformed her into a wicked sorceress, or else a princess with a heart of fragile Dresden china. She fears the onset of another attack of gibbering mania.

The arrival in Moondoona of Nigel's mother opens Part Two, "Wednesday." She and Linda share a mutual but concealed hatred, but she has long known and admired Kay, who confesses to her a love for her son, a married man.

More is revealed about Nigel's past. After his marriage he voyaged with a medical colleague and close friend, Dr. Penleigh ("Pen"), to the uninhabited island, where they set up a colony founded upon the ideal of eugenic breeding of children. But he has agreed with Linda that they must not have offspring; and with terrible irony his wife must observe happy children playing beneath the mountain while she herself is denied motherhood. Then Pen is killed in some sort of riot, during which Nigel is bound and helpless. The colony fails amid scandal and headlines such as "Abominations Practised in the Name of Science." World War I has broken out, and Nigel serves in France before returning to seek peace in the quiet countryside. Linda and Nigel stay together, because he feels sorry for her, and she needs his care. Both her father and her spiderlike uncle have been confined to the asylum. Linda fears her inbred tendency to madness, and despite their denial of parenthood, the couple remain united only by a strange distortion of love. Healthy and eager, Nigel fears "the just and righteous wrath of his ancestors" for failing to hand on the gift of generation.

Young Dr. Marlow, who has come to take an X-ray of Nigel's injured leg, has just read the scientific volume by Nigel reporting on his experiment in improving human genetics. The book arouses his high admiration, although it has been banned by the government. On an impulse, Marlow calls on Linda to report on the patient, and converses with her about the island experiment. She confesses that "sooner or later, if nothing else had done it, I would have wrecked that — lovely thing he made." Fascinated, the young doctor asks if he may return to view a painting of the island colony that Linda possesses.

Linda calls on Kay, and mockingly reports: "He's probably dead by now." The girl rushes to the bedside, to find Nigel feeling better. The pair worry because the wife will be alone in the house during the night, and both have reason to fear that Linda's mania is homicidal.

Part Three, "Thursday," is the longest section of the book. Both Kay and Mrs. Hendon visit the patient. Dr. Marlow returns to see Linda and finds she has spent the night in a lounge chair in the garden. He asks for more details about the island, and we learn that Linda, driven by the biological urge, had become pregnant by the gifted artist D'Aubert. She leads Marlow to the bedroom, and there shows him a painting of genius. D'Aubert has revealed the beauty of the island, but in one corner appears Linda. "Never in his life had anything given him so strong a conception of evil, not as an active malevolence but as an outcast uncleanliness" (121). The work was entitled "Portrait of Linda." Marlow exclaims, "You ought to burn it!" But Linda plans to sell it to an American collector for a large sum, so that Nigel will have his fortunes restored.

Mrs. Hendon recalls that, after the failure of the island colony in 1915, her son served in France as a private, although he could have had a commission, because to him the supreme commandment was "Thou shalt not kill." In his absence, Linda had become wildly promiscuous, and then had returned to her uncle's laboratory. There, in a fit of madness, the uncle had tried to strangle her and had been carried off to an asylum. Mrs. Hendon does not suspect that Linda, in vengeance, had goaded her uncle to attack her in homicidal frenzy.

Marlow is warned by the resident doctor, Bland, that the town is circulating scandalous gossip about his meetings with Linda, and advises that he keep away from the Hendon house. Linda is thus more alone than ever. Through her thoughts, the revelation of events of the night when the experiment collapsed brings a climax to the previously hinted story. Pregnant, she had climbed in the moonlight to a shelf above her island house. She had accidentally fallen through the hillside scrub and a boulder had painfully pinned down her foot. Yet she was able to see a crowd of colonists attack the house with demands that they be disbanded and returned to Australia, to join the forces in 1915 that were enlisting to save England in the war.

Anticipating Edith Cavell, Nigel responds: "Patriotism is not enough." He reminds the rioters of the conditions under which they had come to the island, but one of them taunts him: "You and your conditions! 'Mentally and physically fit!' What about your wife?" Thus Linda becomes the serpent in this utopian Eden.

The rebels tie Nigel to a post and carry away his henchman, Dr. Penleigh, to be killed for some unclear reason. Nigel's wrists are slashed by a woman in the crowd. The stores and medical supplies are burned and the colonists plan to embark for the mainland next morning, leaving the eugenic dream in a shambles.

Linda finally frees herself, although she presumably will have a miscarriage and will always walk with a limp as a result of her foot injury. She cuts Nigel's bonds but can never free him from his doomed, loving bondage to her. After his return, his career blighted because of his overt pacifism, he takes up the burden of trying to keep her sane.

Linda pays a night visit to the invalid, but he drifts into sleep and is unaware that she is seeing him for the last time and, feeling her worthlessness, plans to pass out of his life.

The culmination of the action comes in the brief Part Four, "Friday." Kay, at Nigel's bedside, agrees that "half the people in the world should never have been born at all," and they think of "all the people who should be born and aren't" (188). She declares that it is not too late for him to have the children he desires, and presumably he accepts the offer of herself. He then asks her to go to the hotel and look after his mother, who is threatened with a heart attack.

Linda, exhausted after spending a morning burning all her papers and other treasures, lies on the floor, seeking coolness as a thunderstorm promises to break the growing heat of the past days. Mrs. Hendon arrives in a car, and they face each other, old enemies finally opposed. Linda towers, "vast and powerful," with "all evil gathered gloriously into herself."

Kay, dreaming of marriage with Nigel and planning to call their first boy by her favorite name, Christopher, pursues Mrs. Hendon through the rain to the house where Linda has made her preparations. In a climactic confrontation, Kay rescues the older woman from the murdering hands of Linda, who now knows herself to be incurably insane.

Yet Kay, in her pride in youth and strength, is to know defeat. She promises Linda that Nigel will never hear of the attack. Linda laughs to herself.

She was thinking that this Kay would grab her poor comfortable little happiness with a triumph which she would never realize to be out of all proportion to its worth; bear Nigel's children with blissful pride, never knowing that his truest tenderness would be always for the child to whom he had denied its life. Live with him, long halcyon years, bask in his kindness, his passion, his imperturbable good humour, never dreaming, poor fool, poor brainless little fool, that she had been cheated, tricked, vanquished at the very last! Yes, vanquished, by one who, lame, mad, old, cursed in every way, had still taken with her, when she went, the only years that had really mattered; all his youth, all the glory and turmoil and tragedy that flamed now like brilliant threads through the tapestry of his life, and all his love. . . . (200)

Kay would live with Nigel, always knowing that there was a secret she didn't dare reveal. The witch wife, ironically, wins in the end. Her suicide is the final triumph over a hereditary doom.

As with *Slow Dawning*, the plot of *Prelude to Christopher* was carefully scheduled, and it is a surprise to be told that Mrs. Dark is dominated by her creations. Her husband is reported as saying: "Her work is not built to a preconceived pattern, but is an evolution, an organic growth. For example, in Prelude to Christopher, characters that she expected to be important faded into the background, as the story evolved, and Linda, who began as a secondary character, dominated the book.''² The same interviewer quoted Mrs. Dark as saying:

> Method? I haven't got any. I never know what I am going to write when I start. I know that some writers lay out their books, chapter by chapter, with headings and little plots for each, but I couldn't do that. I never know how my story is going to evolve, what the characters are going to do. Except for The Timeless Land, that is. In that, the whole course of the story, the skeleton, was laid down by history. Some sort of an idea stirs me up to write something. Perhaps a scene, an incident, a song, and the book grows out of it. In the case of Prelude to Christopher, it was Tchaikovsky's Sixth Symphony [a few bars of which were printed on the flyleaf of the first edition]. The book grew out of that. I couldn't possibly tell you how. I follow my characters along and see what they do. It is very harassing, going along blindly and not knowing what will happen next, or whether anything will happen. But it is the only logical way for me to write. (251 - 52)³

Elsewhere she speaks of herself as " 'the most downtrodden, bullied, humble puppet of my characters as ever was!' ''⁴ And again, "Prelude to Christopher she thought over for a year before putting pen to paper. Then, she waited to get 'a grip of the characters,' only to find as she proceeded that they got a grip of her instead. Linda (in this book) took complete control of her own actions, though the other characters flowed more spontaneously. In writing, Mrs. Dark, unlike many authors, who have to rely on technique more than on natural art, does not plan ahead.''⁵

This testimony seem disingenuous. Mrs. Dark is too good an analyst of the minds of others to be self-deluded into thinking that plots which click along section by section can be the result of uncontrolled "evolution." Prelude to Christopher and the other psychological novels that followed are not the work of a writer who is in danger at any time of painting herself into a corner. What is more likely is that, by pondering a book's plot for some time before the act of writing begins, the author holds it all in mind at once, and each character logically falls into place in the general scheme. The presumably minor role of Linda could not have been maintained in this novel; without her the story would have been merely a tasteless romance between a pretty nurse and an admirable convalescent who added to his other misfortunes an insane wife. Unless the love of

Nigel for that insane wife, and her own progress from girlhood through harrowing maturity, were deeply motivated, the triangle would be incomprehensible. Linda is the central character because she, even more than Nigel, is the one to whom the events of the action are literally matters of life and death. Creation of such a character is more likely to have resulted from wide reading in abnormal psychology textbooks than from listening to Tchaikovsky, although a musical memory could quite believably trigger the act of starting to plot a novel.

The leading male character, Dr. Nigel Hendon, is presumably the chief focus of interest from the opening page. His nature, quite logically, is a mixture of the traits of his parents; his mother is strong in her stout conventionality, but his late father, a hearty Irishman (like Eleanor O'Reilly's father) and "eccentric genius," contributed a wild, passionate streak. Nigel is a healthy and intelligent male who should have healthy and intelligent children. He is a "practical idealist" — a dangerous combination, according to the evil Dr. Paul Hamlin. Nigel wishes the world and its people to be as orderly and rational as a scientist's laboratory. He dreams of a great achievement for humanity and — partly through the wicked support of Hamlin — is able to obtain backing for his colony and operate it for five years. But thereafter he declines in our estimation and allows himself to be chained for more than twenty years to an afflicted and faithless wife. Yet Hendon, self-sentenced for many years to childlessness, is more than a man who married the wrong woman. The reader is deeply concerned about his past and his future, and feels that he has earned happiness with young Kay the nurse.

It is Nigel's wife, however, who commands the most attention. She is sinuous, snakelike, with green eyes, wet-looking black hair, and a masklike mouth — the wicked witch of fairy tales. She limps with a swagger. Yet she has a "beautiful brain." Her madness is intermittent and in the end harms no decent person. Cursed by heredity, she survives only because all her courage was borrowed from her husband's "inexhaustible fund, all her faith constantly replenished from his, all her sanity . . ."(34). When his strength is weakened by illness, she is unable to carry on alone. The reader becomes increasingly convinced of her mania through listening to her thoughts and memories. It is quite true, as several reviewers hint, that the character of Linda does dominate the story, almost eclipsing the rest of the cast.

However, several of the supporting characters are interesting in their own rights. Mrs. Hendon is, perhaps, the typical conventional mother, but a typical mother is needed in a novel about generation. Kay, the blue-eyed, golden-haired, wholesome nurse with her nunlike coif, disdains reforms and martyrdom, "short-cuts to perfected humanity," but is an excellent choice for a mate. She is in love and frankly believes that being in love means having a lover. Their children, beginning with a boy to be named Christopher, will surely be eugenically sound.

Dr. Paul Hamlin is the type of evil scientist, hunchbacked, looking like a spider or a toad, cursed with a sadistic drive. He even lacks a sound body. He gloats ironically. "He had sat there and listened, knowing that Nigel, worshipper of normality, apostle of Eugenics, founder of a colony whose basis was to be the rearing of healthy children from untainted stock, was about to marry a potential lunatic. And he had smiled; he had enjoyed the thought"(49).

Among other persons in the story, young Dr. Marlow, who reads Nigel's suppressed book and is suddenly involved in the Hendon tragedy, is most promising as a provider of secondary suspense, but he is engaged to a respectable young lady and sensibly accepts Dr. Bland's advice to avoid their house.

Quite properly for this sort of novel, the conflict must be an entanglement of two natures — those of the husband and the wife. Even more intense, however, is the conflict within Linda, between survival and thwarted motherhood. The thoughts of lesser personages suitably enhance and add credibility to the thoughts of the two leading characters.

The lack of a wide cast and several subplots is compensated for in this book by the authenticity with which the setting is presented. The country town is so well pictured that one Australian expatriate, the poet John Manifold, huddled around a London gas fire, was able to write: "It was not principally for their human characters that I used to read and reread these early novels of Eleanor Dark [*Prelude to Christopher* and *Sun Across the Sky*], but for the feel of sunlight and the smell of boronia. The characters were living such intensely inward lives, so wrapped in reminiscence and self-analysis, that I didn't find them very good company. Their actions, rare in any case and impelled by a powerful head of emotional steam, were too premeditated, violent, and tragic to strike me as real. But the landscape, the Australianism of the background, that was dinkum!"[6]

*Prelude to Christopher* might be classified today as a novel of suspense, for the release of information is artfully delayed and hinted at, until an ending appears that might have been a foregone conclusion. It also might be a "gothic" tale of a witch woman of homicidal tendencies. Perhaps it is best, however, to put it in the category of the psychological novel, in which the motives and impulses of the main characters provide the mainsprings of action. The stream-of-consciousness method is quite suited to psychological fiction such as this novel and Mrs. Dark's next one, *Return to Coolami*.

In writing *Prelude to Christopher*, Mrs. Dark was clearly faced with two big problems. The first is having a main character, Nigel, spend the entire four days recumbent in a hospital bed, asleep most of the time. A patient rather than an agent, he is only mildly able to direct events. The second difficulty is having the leading woman character a victim of insanity. Many readers do not care to spend time on the behavior of abnormal persons, since one can learn little from them about the motives of ordinary folk. However, the naturalist author in our century has felt impelled not to exclude from fiction the outcast, the criminal, the underprivileged, the defective — and here Eleanor Dark broadened the scope of her country's tradition to include a madwoman as a center of attention. And, of course, Linda is not hopelessly mad until the final pages. Whether she will become so is a further twist of suspense.

From her early writing, especially in the short stories, Eleanor Dark felt that the best way to handle a narrative was to concentrate upon the thoughts of the various characters, thus achieving a certain surgical analysis. By 1934, when *Prelude to Christopher* was published, this focus — for which the term "interior monologue" is preferable to "stream of consciousness" — was no new invention. (Whether the "monologue" is introduced by "he thought" or whether offered directly as a kind of tape-recording of the mind is immaterial; actually its use is no more modern than the soliloquies of the Elizabethan drama, which never were spoken to reflect anything but the authentic thoughts of the character.)

The interior monologue was widely used in the 1930s by many authors who had not read James Joyce or Virginia Woolf. Mrs. Dark, although familiar with both these writers, was not especially enthralled by either, although she recalled with pleasure the probing earlier novels of Aldous Huxley, such as *Antic Hay*. To her, revelation of the thoughts of characters in crises is the main material of fiction, rather than a device assumed as a slick technique for technique's sake.

On the other hand, there was a lengthy time lag in the arrival of

modernistic techniques in Australia, where most of the authors were
amateurs lacking mastery of the psychological method. A perceptive
reviewer of *Return to Coolami* in 1936 noted that the subjective
method "permits naturalness while excluding absolutely all non-
essentials. . . . Perhaps the thing of greatest literary importance
about Mrs. Dark's altogether fine novel is that this author, at least,
steps completely over that time lag. Her novel is perfectly modern —
in its technique, in its form, its psychological concept of character."[7]
Yet as late as 1937 another reviewer could object to the "un-
naturalness" of the interior monologue, and term its utilization a
"ruse."[8]

As her husband has commented, "Many critics . . . thought she
persisted in the use of interior monologue simply to show her vir-
tuosity in employing a difficult technique, and they got quite an-
noyed about it. She used that method because it was, for her, the
simplest and most natural. Anyway, who ever heard of a critic
scolding an author for writing book after book in direct narrative?
Why, then, be peevish when a writer chooses to continue to tell a
story through the thoughts of the characters?"[9] From start to finish,
Eleanor Dark's novels have placed more emphasis upon psychological revelation than upon complications of action, and have
stressed the "why" in addition to the "what."

A further advantage of the psychological method is to arouse and
maintain suspense. If the reader can know only what a character is
thinking, facts may legitimately be withheld which would have to be
revealed at once by the honest author using the objective focus. For
example, just what happened on Nigel's island becomes a question
that increasingly arouses the reader's interest. This early event in the
lives of the characters is alluded to teasingly, but the murder of Pen
by the mob while Linda lies helpless on the hillside is not described
until chapter 22. And we are not quite sure up to the last paragraph
exactly to what rash act Linda's warped brain will drive her.

Another device early used by Mrs. Dark was limiting the running
time of the action to a minimum. In *Prelude to Christopher* the "on-
stage" events are restricted to four days, lending a compression
which has been condemned by some as merely a technical trick
designed to cover up the sensationalism or sentimentality of the
material. "As sophistication of technique is unusual in Australian fiction, this aspect of Eleanor Dark's work has been overpraised,"
writes Professor G. A. Wilkes. "Her craftsmanship, in this early
period, is largely 'slickness.' When a writer like Conrad invokes

time-shift, it is to escape the convention which ordains that in chronological narrative, one event may be treated only once: Conrad wishes to disengage certain happenings and treat them a number of times, from different standpoints, and makes the dislocations for the sake of a more thorough scrutiny. With Eleanor Dark it is otherwise. She uses time-shift to contract the action to the span of four days, because she is aware that this presentation has more impact; the theme is not more completely expressed by the technique, it is simply made more arresting. The same opportunism is seen in her use of thematic symbolism. . . .'"[10] It is hard to see why a writer should be accused of "opportunism" because she practices economy to lend intensity. Aristotle would have agreed with Mrs. Dark on economy of time span. Material which can be compressed into four days should not be spread over five days. In several of the later novels, the clock time is reduced by Mrs. Dark to two days, one day, or the daylight hours alone — not to cover up inadequacies, but to bestow a deliberate unity to the theme and the action.

No defense need be given in future consideration of Eleanor Dark's novels to her use of the interior monologue or the limited span of action time. Rather, here, let us record two recognitions of her powers in this early novel by highly competent reviewers. Nettie Palmer was able to say in 1934 in considering *Prelude to Christopher:* "It is wonderful to come across a novel that is really 'written': one that shows the author well in charge of the paragraphs. . . . She has chosen a theme of more than ordinary difficulty, if not of impossibility: madness suddenly gaining ground in a highly self-conscious intelligence. . . . Off-stage action is notoriously difficult to convey, yet the whole story emerges clearly; and most of the characters. . . . This is a tragic novel that may be understood differently by various readers; it deserves the attention of all of them."[11] Even more laudatory is the comment of Eric Lowe, a fellow novelist and friend: "[*Prelude to Christopher*] remains, for me, the finest work that Eleanor Dark has done. It has strength and beauty. The emotional tension throughout is so great that it is almost unbearable, and the reading of Linda's mental struggle becomes, at times, an actively unhappy experience. The climax is artistically inevitable, and magnificent."[12]

Another novelist, Howard Spring, in a favorable review that named *Prelude to Christopher* the "book of the month" of the London *Evening Standard*,[13] introduced Eleanor Dark to a wider public and brought critical attention to her next book, *Return to Coolami*.

## CHAPTER 4

# Times of Sky and Sun

I N two successive years, Eleanor Dark published psychological novels dealing respectively with a journey into the outback and life in a seaside settlement.

*Return to Coolami* (1936) narrates an automobile trip from Sydney to a country region north of Gulgong — a town recalling the Australian gold rush of the 1850s. Four people ride in the shiny new touring car. The driver, Tom Drew, age fifty-eight, is a successful businessman with an impressive house in the suburb of Balool. He has been married for thirty-seven years to Millicent, who was reared on the lovely inland sheep station of Wondabyne. In the back seat are their son-in-law, Bret Maclean, owner of the neighboring station of Coolami, and their daughter Susan, who has been married to Bret for less than a year. She has been staying with her parents for four months after losing her baby, but now the younger couple are being driven back to Bret's home beyond the Blue Mountains.

A number of varying ideas are introduced in the story, but the main theme seems to be that time can change many relationships once thought to be immutable, and that life is for living. In the penultimate chapter, the young wife Susan tells herself: "Never forget things. Never lose them. Keep them there, however unprepossessing they may be, always under your eye, and make them work for you. For surely . . . that's what all your life is for? All of it, everything that has happened, good and bad, is only the material available to you for the building of your future?" Yet she had "a dreadful momentary sense of frustration because she realized that the joy and fullness of bodily union can never be equaled by a union of the mind. Things interfere." Two people may fuse their spirits, creating a mysterious but far from illusory power called love, but they do not seem "able to create by a mental fusion anything whatever" (303).[1] But this frustration may be overcome by discovering that comradeship may provide many compensations lacking in a passionate affair.

## I  *Love Can Blossom*

The interrelationships of the four travelers during the three-hundred-mile journey through eastern New South Wales are revealed not only by the events of their trip but, once more, by introspective flashbacks that uncover the highlights of the past emotion-filled year.

The younger couple are on the verge of divorce, but Bret says, rationally, "I do like you, I admire you, I want you, and I want children" (88). He doesn't understand "love," and doesn't think he wants to. It seems to him to be a sixth sense that he lacks. Susan has agreed to go back to Coolami (the name means "birthplace of heroes") and live with Bret, although there is a flaming sword between them. The crux of their alienation is that, whereas Susan has always devotedly loved Bret, he has married her out of pity and nurses a prideful hatred of her because, at the age of nineteen, she yielded in a romance with his beloved young brother Jim. When, pregnant for two months by Jim, Susan in Sydney is told by Bret that Jim has been killed by a car when on his way to a rendezvous with the girl, she yields to his quixotic plea that they marry in order to give the baby a parenthood. When the baby dies soon after birth, the logical reason for staying together disappears. The only bar to their full happiness together is Bret's stubborn refusal to yield to Susan's youth, flaming beauty, and fervent affection. If they are to find a full life together, this barrier must be worn away by time and events. Through two days and a night, during which the reader lives with a couple that engage in a sort of ritual love dance, a satisfying ending is wrought for them. Susan's wit and dignity are more than a match for Bret's outward reserve. The main plot question is merely: When will Bret make his wife truly his wife? This story, then, is a charming one for readers who find it more pleasant to journey than to arrive.

The conflict between Drew and his wife Millicent is less critical. She had eloped with him from her country home when she had known him, a striving bank clerk, for less than a week. She had seen his success in business as an effort to please her by buying everything he thought she might wish, whereas she yearned only to return to the comfortable station life of her youth. The gleaming new automobile is a symbol of their city status, and in it the foursome starts out on the journey very early one morning, over a winding road that Drew has never before driven. He in his turn must be converted — to the possibility that success in a city career is not a true fulfillment of their marital happiness.

This brief statement of the plot of *Return to Coolami* does not do justice to the cleverness with which events of the journey are interwoven with roving flashes of reverie in the minds of the four travelers, recalling in shifting scenes the motivating influences upon their relationships.

The car leaves the suburbs, ascends the river west of Sydney, passes Parramatta, and climbs the ridges into the heart of the Blue Mountains. Near a famed lookout spot they have a late breakfast, and Bret and Susan enact another episode in their love duel. Beyond Katoomba, on a dangerous incline, the driver loses control and the car skids off the road. "They were facing for a fraction of a second the high rock wall, then the slope down which they had just come, with the crazy wheel marks of their passage standing out like part of a too-long continued nightmare. Then there was nothing in front of them but a distant glimpse of tree-tops and a white-painted railing which didn't look strong enough —" (118). Fortunately, the car recovers from the brink but is mired in a muddy ditch, and Bret and Susan walk to the next village to bring a rescue vehicle. The shock of sudden confrontation with death has brought each journeyer into a more realistic frame of mind. The main concern of the younger couple is the fear that the prosperous homeplace, Coolami, would fall into weak hands.

Near Mudgee the party stops beside a willow-fringed creek for another roadside meal. Bret recalls that he had once intruded upon Jim and Susan when they were picnicking in this spot, and the loss of his brother, who loved Coolami as much as did Bret himself, is keener than ever. Toward nightfall the party arrives at the dilapidated station called Kalangadoo, south of Mudgee, which is managed — badly — by Susan's brother Colin and his wife Margery. This third couple also have a large problem. Colin had gone off to World War I at the age of eighteen and, unlike the sturdier Bret, had suffered the aftereffects of sustained combat. Taking refuge in alcohol, he had become a pathetic failure. That morning, fearing the arrival of family, he had gotten drunk, pushed his three-year-old son Richard, and driven off in anger. Margery settles the visitors in the run-down house and confesses to Bret that she fears Colin has climbed to a secret cave halfway up the side of looming Mount Jungaburra.

Bret sets out alone to find Colin, whose car, with a loosened brake, has been shattered in a ravine. Once again, as in *Prelude to Christopher*, a critical episode is played on a moonlit mountainside. Bret finds Colin, slightly injured, and with the aid of a rope he has brought the two begin the dangerous descent of the rocks. At a hazardous spot, illuminated by the lights of the Drew automobile, Bret is amazed to encounter Susan, who has been familiar with this ascent during rambles with her brother. Together they get Colin home, and in the morning he is able to pretend that nothing has happened. But his escapade has strengthened his will to improve his life, and thus quickly the subplot of the Colin Drew family is brought to a solution.

Bret and Susan are closer now than brother and sister, but the question of their future as a couple and as prospective parents is still a hazard that might lead to tragedy. The second day of the journey opens after twenty-three chapters of narrative devoted to the first day. Bret recalls his wedding and virginal honeymoon, when he began to feel that the marriage might at least yield companionship and trust, if not romantic love. Reminders of the liaison between Jim and Susan do not now arouse his hatred of her. He suspects that her feeling for Jim was a weak reflection of her unsuspected, deeper love earlier for himself. "He thought that probably she was right to insist so on her relationship with Jim. That uncompromising determination of hers to stress at all times the strange parallel of his present attitude to her with her past attitude to his brother might be, according to her code of honesty and pride, her only possible course" (269). Irritated by his unhabitual preoccupation with introspection since his marriage, he concludes that "emotions needed exercise just like your muscles," and breaks the news to his wife that love is a remedy for emotional constipation.

The remaining miles separating the party from Coolami pass quickly. At another roadside picnic, Bret realizes in a moment that love can blossom overnight like a flower. "He didn't know, or care really, how long there had been accumulating in him the feeling towards her which only today had been fused into the one grateful and beneficent gladness which now pervaded him. . . . He didn't know why or how it was that he should find he could remember Jim without anger or resentment" (297). For both of them now, Coolami will be their home and their future.

## II  "*So Many Unnecessary Barriers*"

The parents have also been developing a crisis. Tom Drew, the self-satisfied city man, has awakened to the charm of the open countryside and the appeal of endless roads leading westward. Colin has told him that Wondabyne, Millicent's old home, is suddenly for sale. With ten or twenty years of active life still ahead of him, Drew decides to purchase Wondabyne, restore its graciousness with the help of Colin and Margery, and explore the outback world with Millicent, whose dream through the years had always been a return to Wondabyne.

The brief journey in time had bridged an enormous distance in human feelings. "A funny journey it had been," Bret concludes on the dark steps of his hereditary home. "After all, in a sense, he'd run amok himself. And yet nothing had happened. They had all been calm and civil and matter-of-fact and very nearly monosyllabic as one usually is. . . . Words were heavy things, tearing, destroying things like stones flung through a cobweb." He puts out his hand to touch his wife's, prolonging the "moment for which he now felt he had been waiting all his life"(318 - 19).

Bret Maclean is obviously the person to whom the events of the journey mean the most. He has been devoted, through all his thirty-five years, to the welfare of Coolami, a heritage spreading over seventy thousand acres. His devotion also to his young brother Jim — the only person who shared with him a dedication to Coolami — was a dominant trait, and the death of Jim plunged him into his most serious crisis. Overcoming his love of Jim by his growing love of Susan might seem a simple emotional change, but the complications of this change make the story. At the end, Bret realizes that indulging in "highbrow dabbling in psychological bunk" (270) is not for him. He must take the good things that time brings, and consciously enjoy them.

Susan is a small, brown-eyed, red-haired spitfire of twenty-one, who has had and lost a baby and has engaged in a convenient marriage. Quite unlike her undemonstrative parents, she is all verve and energy. She is more than a match for Bret in wit and decisiveness, and the reader is pleased when at last she attains to the life of a station owner's happy mate. She realizes that her attraction to Jim had really been a reflection of a deeper affection for the older brother, whom he greatly resembled. Seldom do we worry that plucky Susan cannot take care of herself, even when she is bearing the child of a lover who died in a street accident.

Tom Drew's conversion from a city businessman to a potential owner of a country station is motivated through his adventures as the driver of a touring car on the western roads. The possibility dawns on him that the people of the outback might enjoy freer lives than those in the metropolis, and that his wife had never been so happy as when she roved the paddocks of Wondabyne. His fresh spirit is symbolized by the dancing silver figure he had bought to put on his radiator cap — an image ever pointing forward into the beckoning unknown. His wife Millicent, aged fifty-six, is an understanding mother who is able to refrain from interfering with the lives of her children, while at the same time making quiet arrangements for them to fulfill their alien concerns. She also has her deepest yearnings suddenly granted at the end of the journey. The couple at Kalangadoo — Colin and Margery — are sketched more briefly, and their problem is on the way to solution overnight. The novel frugally avoids including any more characters of concern other than the six upon whom the focus is centered throughout.

One of the chief charms of this book is the varied settings depicted during the trip across eastern New South Wales. The suburb yields to the Great Western Road, and the party pauses for a meal on the brink of a famed scenic spot quite near the home of Eleanor Dark at Katoomba. Thereafter we are given views of the fertile countryside beyond the barrier of the Blue Mountains, and the landscape of Coolami — "the great valley glowing with opalescent light, the wheat-fields quivering and flowing to the current of a vagrant breeze, the river like a mirror beneath a green deluge of weeping willows" (314).

Tom Drew's curiosity about the men who found the way over the mountains and built the highway is aroused, and the author's remarks about these pioneers foreshadow the writing of a novel, *No Barrier*, that was to appear seventeen years later. Millicent recalls that Bret's mother had domesticated at Coolami the wild plants of the west — boronia, gee bung, tea-tree, malaleuca, eriostemon. The novel does, in John Manifold's phrase, recall "the feel of sunlight and the smell of boronia." The route of the riders is based on several journeys by the Darks into the back country. Once they were accompanied by Eric Lowe, who wrote: "On one such expedition we drove to the Warrumbungle Range, and stayed there to climb. I like to think that this trip was responsible for *Return to Coolami*, or at least that the way we took was molded into the road traveled by Bret and Susan."[2]

Since *Return to Coolami* is mainly a romance in which the most abnormal emotions do not intrude, the psychological interest is less profound than in *Prelude to Christopher*. However, as in the earlier novel, the probing of subjective feelings is the main method used to reveal the action (for again, most of the events of importance have occurred before the curtain rises on the stage). Reviewers this time were able to appreciate much better the author's self-education in modernist methods of narration. A perceptive critic wrote, concerning the overcoming of the time lag in Australia's use of such methods: "Perhaps the thing of greatest literary importance about Mrs. Dark's altogether fine novel is that this author, at least, steps completely over that time lag. Her novel is perfectly modern — in its technique, in its form, its psychological concept of character. . . . Its modernness — by which is meant its being directly in tune, in the beat of the life-rhythm of this present time — gives it an importance in Australian literary effort which seems very great today."[3]

Other reviews were equally laudatory. Three American comments may be quoted. "But part of the book's value lies in its sympathetic presentation of the pitfalls that beset kind and honest people caught in the miserable consequences of their own good intentions. And the mental twistings and turnings of Susan and Bret invariably are understandable; neither is wholly right nor wholly wrong, unreasonable nor morbid. They remain likable young persons in a mess and it becomes important to the reader to see them out of it."[4]

Alfred Kazin, author of a standard work on American fiction, wrote:

> What is good in *Return to Coolami* is due to a free-swinging intensity that hits more often than it misses, and the curious excitement that pervades the book does not depend on the turn of plot or the clash of ideas but results from a steady investigation of character that is vitalized by unusually keen insights. . . . What emerges are dynamic emotions, emotions in the process of being changed or fulfilled or merged, not people who have been delineated so well that the novelist has only to prod them along to produce the effect of motion. . . . It is a significant indication of Miss Dark's talent that her novel should possess the constant interest that it does, or that there should be so much pulsating life between so many unnecessary barriers.[5]

A woman reviewer concluded: "The characters are interesting and intelligent, warm-hearted and loving, and the author has depicted them with skill and understanding."[6]

An Australian reviewer appreciated especially the treatment of setting: "There are many fine pictures of Australian scenes throughout the novel, and there is no stressing of atmosphere or historic facts. Australia is at last being treated in literature as an established and normal background. The people in this story are natural and logical in their outlook and actions. The writing is unaffected and efficient; the style, if not distinguished, is certainly not either slipshod or over-elaborate."[7]

*Return to Coolami,* like *Prelude to Christopher,* captured the prized medal of the Australian Literary Society of Melbourne in 1936.

## III  *A Painting of Sunlight*

Apparently a random chronicle of a day's happenings at a seaside resort, *Sun Across the Sky* (1937) is actually a tightly woven fabric. This is a day of decisions, of crises, among half a dozen people whose lives clash or come together. Unity is maintained by using the sun as a symbol.

The action begins before dawn, when Sir Frederick Gormley, now fifty-five, the tycoon who has created the new, shiny seaside town of Thalassa, awakens with a stomachache resulting from indulgence, and ponders once more how he can wipe out the fishing village across the lagoon, a "slum" on land held by the poet Kavanagh, who refuses all offers to sell. When the first rays come, the man of money shields his eyes and damns the sun.

The next chapter — usually each chapter focuses upon the mind of another character than the previous one — shows the waking of Dr. Oliver Denning, who awaits with joy the sun's coming. But his wife Helen, also waking, does not understand this association of creative inspiration with sunlight, and instead turns her adoration inward, toward her long, metallic golden hair. Her seven years of marriage, she realizes, have been "a mental and a physical rape" (28). She plans to use her day preparing a bridge party. Oliver senses that she suffers from "vitaphobia" — fear of life itself.

Lois Marshall, widowed painter who has just returned to her home on the hillside, gets up early, lies on the lawn, and is inspired to work on a picture of a gnome, hammering out Rhine gold in a cavern, horribly shut away from the sun. Unlike her writer husband, who had left her comfortably off through income from carefully planned potboilers, she creates impulsively, finding that the essence of beauty is its elusiveness.

Starting on his rounds, Oliver observes the sun-worshippers in the park and on the beach and feels that "his friend the sun was now in complete and undisputed possession" (52). While he is pondering the effect the Australian sun will have on the development of a new,

lean, tanned race, a man is attacked by a shark. Oliver races him to
the hospital. He is Bill Armstrong, and he is the father of the child
that elfin Maeve Kavanagh, daughter of the poet, will bear in
defiance of the laws of society. Oliver is upheld by a natural op-
timism, a challenge to tragedy, as if, his wife feels, "only by standing
up and defying life to come on and do its worst could he find the full
measure of his vitality" (76). He is also supported by a firm belief in
the medical credo and by an appreciation of beauty created by art.

Oliver attends to Sir Frederick's bellyache but refuses to condemn
the dwellers in the fishing village as unsanitary or dirty. "They're
drenched in sun from morning till night and there's no dirt near
them — only clean sea sand" (111). On his way back to other
patients he gives a lift to the flirtatious Myra Waterford, Gormley's
mistress, who has at least one virtue — she loves the sun "better than
anything." Behind them, in Sir Frederick's mind arises the germ of a
scheme to rid the community of the unsightly fishing shacks.

Oliver spends an hour with old Kavanagh at his beach cottage,
warns him about his weak heart, and enjoys beer from a German
stein along with an outpouring of divine conversation. Kavanagh is
not a man of the sun, but rather of firelight and moonlight: "A
strange nocturnal being, a huge shadow walking and muttering to
itself, tearing out of itself with agony and toil some thought shaped
at last into immortal words" (116).

Arriving home for lunch, Oliver catches his wife asleep at the table
and gently, hopefully kisses her forehead. She responds to his touch
with terror and revulsion. Later, he asks her if she would like a
divorce, but she has a Victorian horror of scenes and scandal, of seeing her name in the newspaper.

Called away to an emergency operation on Herb Sayers, cornet-
playing salvationist and vegetable hawker living in the old village,
Oliver chats with the hospital matron. He is aghast at her acceptance
of the doctrine of joyless self-denial. "Not self-denial, but self-
expression," is his reaction to her view of humanity. "The two
priceless qualities which gave him ascendancy over the animal — his
power to think, his power to laugh" (226).

Donning his bathing suit to take a much needed and relaxing
swim, Oliver ponders "the transformations wrought between sunrise
and sunset of any day" (241). He is unaware that Gormley has sent
orders to an arsonist who is in his power — orders to set fire to the
dry hillside above the fishing village and wipe out the cottages that
deface Thalassa's landscape. Sir Frederick dallies with Myra,

meanwhile watching through the window for the first tongues of flame.

Oliver relishes the challenge of the sea, feeling that "it must be surely very necessary to the moral health of the human animal that he should risk his life — well, at least once every six months!" (265). He suddenly decides to call on Lois, whom he has not seen since the night three months before which they had gloriously spent together. The picture she has just painted expresses what Oliver has been thinking all day, and prefigures the main theme of the book. "That everything of good in the world is eternally yours so long as it — and you — remain free. That sunlight you've painted is warmth, and power, and strength and beauty, but the gnome can't hold it. That's so strange to him that he's frightened now. He's resentful. He's used to grabbing. But some day he'll be content just to sit in it, and absorb it, and make himself a part of it" (285).

A crisis has arisen. When they fell in love before, Lois had not seen Oliver's beautiful wife, and she knows how much Oliver loves anything beautiful. But when she hears that Helen does not care about holding him, she agrees to let Oliver return that night.

### IV   *The Crisis of Oliver*

Strom, the arsonist, meanwhile has set ablaze the dead blackberry bushes on the hillside, which have been killed with an inflammable chemical. The resulting holocaust sweeps down on the fishing village. Myra, in Sir Frederick's arms, notes from his behavior that he has arranged the fire, and rushes down to help the villagers driven from their homes by the advancing flames. She finds Kavanagh struggling to haul a chest from a neighbor's house across the road from his own. Stricken by a heart attack, the giant poet crashes to the ground. Oliver, who has driven madly to the scene, takes Kavanagh's body to the hospital but is unable to save him. The flames, crossing the road, are now menacing Kavanagh's home and his precious pile of original poems. At least the doctor can try to rescue for humanity these outpourings of genius! And in a tense climax, aided by a repentant Myra, he does so, winding up in bed in his own hospital but looking forward to "another sunrise — another day." Thus the story ends.

The chief text for *Sun Across the Sky* — although many other ideas are adumbrated in the minds of its people — seems to be that from the Preacher: "The sun also ariseth, and the sun goeth down, and hasteth to the place where he arose." The final paragraph in-

cludes Oliver's optimistic exclamation to himself: "To despair —
with all the richness which this day had poured into him! With all
the unlimited possibilities of uncountable tomorrows!" (336). This
theme is reinforced by the symbolism. The gnome in Lois's painting, grabbing for gold in the dark, is an image of the Gormleys, but
the rational spirits who open their hearts to the daily messages of
beauty and freedom and love are those who make man more human.

*Sun Across the Sky* is a novel of affirmation of life, comparable to
many other books in the Australian tradition, and reveals the author
as a true Australian, a sun-worshipper. "It is symbolical, I think,"
writes Professor Tom Inglis Moore, "that so many of our writers, especially the poets, invoke the sun in the titles of their books. . . . This
affirmation is not unalloyed. The sun causes the desolation of
drought as well as the joy of the morning or the content in 'the hot,
gold hush of noon.' We have seen that a distinct note of sombreness
runs through both the society and its literature. But we also saw this
was a mood, not a metaphysic: that it rarely deepened into an out-
right pessimism. The major note is the affirmative one, held firmly
by the main line of writers."[8] Eleanor Dark thus holds out hope to
the end for honest people. "Another sunrise — another day."

A less obtrusive symbol than the sun is the idea of captivity — a
word that appears frequently and is usually attached to the
wrongdoers in the cast: Maeve, Gormley, Strom, and Mavis before
her redemption. They are "caught," and victims of the captivity
which is the opposite of the freedom of spirit advocated by Oliver,
who says: "Oh, God, that word 'captivity,' how it thrusts its head up
at you out of all your thoughts" (140). "And yet it wasn't their fault.
Captivity again!" (177). And earlier, almost echoing a manifesto:
"Born free yet everywhere in chains!" (59).

Among the group whose adventures are covered during the
critical day, three men are most prominent. They are Sir Frederick
Gormley, "self-made" man of business; Dr. Oliver Denning, man of
medicine; and Patrick Nicholas Kavanagh, poet. Gormley, whose
name suggests his loathsome nature (a dialect word, "gormless,"
means "lacking in comprehension or awareness") is an unredeemed
rascal, risen by theft and blackmail from his slum boyhood. His only
conscience is his elder sister. He is dominated by three urges — for
power, food, and women — and power for him comes from money.
When faced with Kavanagh, a man unmoved by the offer of money
— when dismissed from attention if a line of poetry comes into that
man's head, Gormley's response is fear and a rationalized desire for

vengeance at the slight. Yielding joyously to the needs of the flesh is acceptable for Oliver, one understands, but Gormley's cavortings with his mistress, Myra Waterford, can only be vile. When the capitalist meets his dramatic doom by being the target of a suicidal collision with the car driven by Strom, his rebellious creature, Gormley's last thought is that the fire did not bring him a victory, but a defeat by Kavanagh. The reader wastes no pity on Sir Frederick. We may understand him, but we do not forgive.

Dr. Denning is the person on whom the focus is most steady during the day, and to whose preoccupations one is closest. He is a heroic figure, a bringer of alleviation and compassion, a man who comes close to death in the end just to salvage a bundle of poems from destruction. Comparable in many ways to Dr. Nigel Hendon in *Prelude to Christopher,* Oliver has the rationality of the scientist and the humanity of the general practitioner. He basks in the enchantment of Kavanagh's personality and sacrifices himself for the community and for art. His crisis, previous to the concluding adventure in which he rescues the Kavanagh manuscripts, is having to choose between remaining with his beautiful but frigid wife, whom he married out of a desire to protect her, or committing adultery with the widowed Lois, the instinctive artist, "a rather stocky young woman with a brown skin and straight brown hair and no kind of features to speak of" (168). When the fire begins to rage, both Lois and Helen disappear from the scene, and the salvaging of the poetry is aided by a reformed Myra Waterford. But one concludes that Oliver and Lois are right for each other (they are to be met later in *Waterway*), and Helen will have to find another shelter where her need for protection can be handled — institutionally, if required.

### V   *"Accepting Life in Its Fullness"*

There is little doubt from the start that Lois will win. She has returned to the town with her daughter and has started again to paint her "allegorical" canvases expressive of the need of humanity to seek the sunshine. She is elvish and impulsive, and filled with a pagan joy of life. Helen we dislike from the start — her fussiness, her worry about appearances, her worship of that little god, "the right thing." She had leaned upon an elder sister until that protector's death, and then transferred the need to the doctor who had seen her through that difficult time. She thinks she loves Oliver, and sees no use for "the addition of those crude, those undignified, those revolting and ridiculous antics in which she could not bring herself to share" (230). Yet her husband really couldn't give her protection, because "the very essence of their relationship," like that in most marriages, "was not shelter but exposure and vulnerability, not protection but combined endeavor" (233). Oliver "liked to take life in armfuls, while she could only bear to touch it with her fingertips" (231). Even with her blond beauty, Helen is no match for Lois the artist. Like Kavanagh, Lois is a creator. As Oliver puts her feelings into words for her: "[the creator is] not simply a creator of things — of beauty or of terror — but a creator of creations. He's a fire that lights a thousand other fires. . . . Kavanagh made me think of it. It doesn't really matter that nine-tenths of mankind never realizes the power and influence of a man like that. It's there" (280 - 81).

Lois easily attracts Oliver, as does Kavanagh. In many ways the spirit of Kavanagh pervades the book and lends it additional unity. He seldom appears on stage directly — mainly at his death — and we never share his thoughts as we do those of many others who are influenced by him. His brilliant conversation must be taken on trust, for no words of his are quoted. But he is the most real character in *Sun Across the Sky*, and the reason may be that he is quite comparable to a real person known to Australian literary circles.

One agrees that there is a difference between a character in a novel and a flesh-and-blood person. None the less, there are too many resemblances between Kavanagh and one of Mrs. Dark's friends to be accidental. Christopher John Brennan, who had given her a copy of his poems when she was fourteen, was generally considered in his lifetime to be the Australian poet closest to world stature. His scholarship was massive; his life was tragic. He earned an M.A. degree at Sydney University at the age of twenty-one and then studied in Germany. He returned to his *alma mater* in 1908 as a teacher of modern languages but in 1925, owing partly to alcoholism and marital difficulties, he resigned from his post as Associate Professor of German and Comparative Literature. Before his death in Sydney in 1932 he lived at Newport Beach, on the peninsula north of the town, on a tract of land later developed into seaside homes.

Brennan was a master of conversation and a poet whose verse and prose is still being collected and studied. "His personality was Johnsonian," runs a modern anthology. "He was more than six feet in height and built in proportion. His presence was formidable, his eyes piercing, his nose monumental, his pipe big enough to roast a quarter of a pound of black tobacco at a filling."[9] Kavanagh is a brother to Brennan, even to the nose and the pipe — "a pipe so vast that seeing it alone you might have thought it not meant for human use, but in his mouth beneath the aggressive majesty of his nose it became fitting and subordinate." As for his power of conversation, "Laughter thundered out of him, rich and Rabelaisian. Speech was no longer a mere medium of communication — it was an art — a black art — a magic with which unguessed miracles could be wrought. Imps, devils and satyrs came to his summons — the world and the nether-world, the firmament and all its angels were the playthings of his speech" (114). The flyleaf of *Sun Across the Sky* contains three quatrains by Brennan, whose personification as Kavanagh the poet brings the strongest unity of characterization to a novel that otherwise might have been a collection of less immortal personages.

The reception of this novel was generally favorable. "The story and the characterization emerge with astonishing clarity from the profuseness of the writing, just as, constructively, the diffuse grouping gives so entirely a sense of the place."[10] Several Sydney reviewers, however, were still bothered by the use of the interior monologue. "Miss Dark still indulges over-much in introspection," ran the *Morning Herald* notice. Yet, "The characterization and manipulation of time-shifts indicate that Miss Dark is a careful craftsman."[11] Again, "These events are not communicated directly to the reader but through what purport to be the reflections of the characters . . . the effect, besides slowing the action appreciably, is to postulate several characters with equal introspective powers exercising them at great length and on the same day with extraordinary aptness to the author's need — a not very natural proceeding."[12]

American reviewers were lukewarm. Louise M. Field did remark that "the opening portions of the book, especially the delineation of Helen's character, are promising, leading the reader to expect a far better novel than *Sun Across the Sky* eventually proves."[13] Lorine Pruette wrote: "There are many good touches in the novel, glimpses of the sea and the land. . . . Lois is an engaging creature, if not precisely believable, while Myra, Sir Frederick's mistress, is done with genuine economy. Miss Dark writes well enough, and when she gets to the climax shows she can present rapid flowing action without telling what everybody is thinking."[14]

A later and more considered judgment labels this novel more "deft" than the earlier ones. "The characters are more subtle, their relationships require more skill in the handling, and the events are, except for a fire at the last, fewer and more commonplace. . . . It is an expert, experienced novel. It is so easy to read that it is not until half-way through that one begins to take note of what is being done. From the earlier novels to this the tendency has been for the author to take over, especially in the introspective musings of characters. Here the assumption is more or less complete. So that we have a series of comments on the importance of accepting life in its fullness, and on the sterility of fear and of resistance to experience."[15]

A year after *Sun Across the Sky*, Eleanor Dark published another novel, *Waterway*, in which the limited number of characters in earlier works is replaced by a larger cast with varied interests, but again the action is restricted to the events of a single day.

## CHAPTER 5

# Time of Travail

ELEANOR DARK'S fourth novel to be published in five years — *Waterway* (1938) — appeared not many months before the outbreak of World War II, and in it echo a number of foreboding rumblings of a second holocaust in a generation. "Failure of Peace Talks" reads Professor Channon in his newspaper, and he muses: "Well, presently perhaps, that greyish patch which was Europe would burst into smoke and flame." Then dreams of inheriting the earth must fail, like peace talks, "because the first principles of life are much too simple to be taken seriously by creatures who had developed a sophisticated intelligence at the expense of a fundamental wisdom" (139).[1]

Australia is still far enough away from Europe, though, to buy time for other concerns than immediate war. The apparent theme of *Waterway* is that conflict between people of great wealth and those of creative, cultural natures should be resolved in favor of those who are not shackled by material possessions. This interpretation is justified by Lesley Channon's dilemma in choosing to marry either Sim Hegarty or Roger Blair, confronted as she is by the misery of her elder sister, who had wedded a wealthy philistine. This dilemma is resolved, however, two-thirds of the way through the story, and it is evident that further illuminations of life's meaning are still to be made.

A number of varied opinions, in fact, crowd the pages of *Waterway*. The author's strong views at times interfere with the progress of the plot, but are usually suitable to the nature of each person who contemplates his position. This novel marks a notable change from the earlier ones, in which broad opinions were seldom indulged. The psychological novel has now also become the novel of ideas.

The main idea, possibly, emerges in the last few pages. Oliver

Denning, general practitioner in a Sydney suburb, views Sydney
Harbour at sunset. A century and a half have passed since the region
was "invaded" by Europeans in 1788. The conflict between the land
and turbulent humanity is still going on. "But in the end, he found
himself thinking, the land will win, the land must always win. One
generation resisted it, crying aloud of exile. Others, following,
denied it with always dwindling strength, but the land is eternal and
it can wait. . . . Its rule is aloof and dispassionate — not an enmity,
but a discipline with which to mould and drive its people, hurt them,
gladden them, terrify or exhilarate them, kill or save them so that
they must become, whether they wish it or not, shaped to some
pattern which will make them one with it at last" (444 - 45). The
author's interest in the events of the first settlement of Sydney,
shown casually in *Waterway*, presage the historical trilogy that
would begin with Eleanor Dark's next novel, *The Timeless Land.*

An introductory note to *Waterway* states that "although some of
the events described in Part IV are based upon real happenings in
November, 1927, all the characters in the book are imaginary." Mrs.
Dark also helpfully includes a list of "main characters" that adds up
to sixteen. All these characters, who in their various roles enact the
themes, are introduced, at least briefly, in Part I, "The Sunrise."

Dr. Oliver Denning, who was the leading figure in *Sun Across the
Sky*, opens the action with a predawn professional call — to deliver a
baby goat for an Italian farmer. Oliver and his second wife, the
former Lois Marshall, have recently moved to the eastern Sydney
suburb of Watson's Bay, named for a pioneer sailor and harbor-
master. Oliver views the spreading shores of Port Jackson, which had
been settled by the First Fleet exactly one hundred and fifty years
before the date of publication of *Waterway*, and pictures himself a
bearded, black-skinned aboriginal viewing this scene, member of a
"brave and ancient race fading slowly to extinction" (12). The sight
of the red roofs of the modern inhabitants reminds him of his
neighbors in the suburb — the Arthur Sellmans, Professor Channon,
and Channon's two daughters. The elder daughter, Winifred, is
married to Sellman but is in love with her next-door neighbor, the
widower Ian Harnett, father of two small boys. The younger
daughter, Lesley, as the reader is to learn, is courted by Sim Hegarty, handsome younger son of a wealthy merchant family, and by
Roger Blair, impoverished editor of a radical, utopian journal. Then,
comfortably, Oliver's thoughts return to his artist wife, Lois, and her
young daughter Chloe.

The scene shifts to the bedroom of Arthur Sellman, the type of philistine businessman who feels that he can buy his wife's continued affection by material things. He has falsely accused her of adultery with Harnett, and the previous night, returning from a boozy stag party, he had locked her with himself in his bedroom. He gives her the key but refuses a divorce, saying that if she demands one he will refuse to let her see again her beloved blind little daughter Brenda.

Lorna Sellman, Arthur's sister, is awakened in a nearby bedroom by her brother's loud words. A fading ash blond, sharing Arthur's shallowness, she thinks of Sim Hegarty, who had once come close to proposing to her but who now was pursuing Lesley Channon. Lorna, a society butterfly, recalls the gossip that Professor Channon had resigned his chair at the university just in time to avoid being dismissed as a radical. She thinks that Winifred is a failure as Arthur's wife because she refuses the usual round of social duties and associates with Harnett and the Dennings.

Ian Harnett has also been awakened by Arthur's rage, and in frustration, suffering from a psychosomatic case of neuralgia, has walked along the harbor to the monument to Robert Watson on South Head. He recalls the origin of his attraction to Winifred, who likes his two sons as well as their father. The boys greet Ian and accompany him home. They pass Oliver on his doorstep, returning to his own house. Oliver goes back to bed after a chat with Chloe, his step-daughter, but Lois wakes and recalls the crisis at the time of the fire in the seaside village of Thalassa, as told in *Sun Across the Sky*.

The scene shifts to the spacious home of Lady Hegarty, the aging widow of Sir James, hardware tycoon. This day will bring the wedding of her elder son, George. Sim, who has just left to swim in the cove, will be best man.

Below South Head, in a rickety shack, Jack Saunders, son of a poor fisherman, prepares a meager lunch and then descends the cliff to the flat rock below The Gap. He enjoys working at physical tasks but has been unemployed for two years. He bears a hatred for all wealthy people, and recalls with bitterness his boyhood friendship with Sim Hegarty, who had been given everything in life and still enjoyed a glamorous existence.

Sim and Roger Blair swim together and contrast their views of life's goals. Roger is an impatient Socialist who despises philanthropists and feels that all should share equally in the good things of the world. Roger accuses Sim of being "too busy enjoying life to think about it." But Sim's recent affair with freethinking Lesley, as well as his recollection of boyhood friendship with Jack Saunders, has caused him for the first time to consider seriously his duty to society.

Roger returns to his humble boardinghouse, reflecting that the journal he runs will probably fail soon for lack of money, although wealthy people waste much of it in futile pleasure while spiritual and cultural values are despised. He fears that Australia is "doomed by custom and apathy to remain for ever nothing but a vast producing machine of goods for export" (87). He is somewhat cheered by a long, encouraging letter from Professor Channon, but Channon counsels patience and says that the greatest goal should be international brotherhood. Roger faces the day with continuing faith in the power of journalism.

In Part II, "The Cove," nearly all the principal persons visit the beach below the houses during the morning. Professor Channon and Lesley swim before she and Harnett join the crowd that catch the ferry to the city. The two Harnett boys swim along with blind Brenda. Lorna chats with Winifred on the sand as an excuse to swim out to the raft later, to spend an hour luring Sim. Lady Hegarty also decides to join her son, although she has not visited the beach for some five years. During office hours, Dr. Oliver Denning attends Professor Channon (who is compassionately informed that he has a terminal case of cancer) and Jack Saunders, who has injured his fingers in a fall on the cliff path below The Gap. Oliver and Lois manage a swim together, and Lois tells Winifred that the Dennings' cook will take the three small children on an outing to the Zoo and then put them on the ten-to-five-o'clock ferry from the city back to Watson's Bay. Typically, Arthur Sellman has not visited the beach, but goes to his office in a Packard. He excuses himself from attending the wedding of George Hegarty but insists that Winifred represent the family. He is angry when she refuses, and threatens reprisals.

Part III is properly labeled "The City." Saunders has drifted there idly. Lorna has a beauty treatment and a manicure, and plans to buy a new hat to wear at the society wedding. Lesley is at work in the Library of New South Wales, reading historical materials in preparation for writing another short story to earn some income. Harnett and Blair start off to lunch together, but they encounter Lesley in the Botanical Gardens, and Harnett leaves the couple to pass the afternoon in conversation.

The wedding goes off well, with Sim as his brother's best man, but Lady Hegarty has a fainting spell and is left to rest in a small room in the church. Lorna carries off Sim to the reception. Channon visits an art exhibition and chats with Lois, who has put some of her paintings on display. On a mad impulse, Winifred comes to Harnett's office by the Quay, and they decide to steal an hour together on the shore.

The wealthy people leaving the reception in their cars collide with a demonstration of the unemployed in front of Parliament House. Roger and Lesley are caught up in the mob, but she is offered a chance to escape in Sim's car, passing by with Lorna and Sim inside. Lesley was "too practical, too logical to be habitually swayed by emotional symbolism, but she felt a conviction at that moment which nothing in her attempted to deny, that here and now her choice must be made. The easy escape into Sim's moving car, the blessed physical relaxation into upholstered comfort and security were also, in a cold light of revelation, another kind of escape" (298). Remaining in the crowd with Roger's arm around her, however, was "the real escape, the only escape, by endurance and achievement, into peace." She had made her decision between two opposing kinds of lovers.

Jack Saunders, dragged along by the crowd, in an angry response aggravated by damage to his injured hand, hurls a beer bottle at the head of a publishing magnate in a car, and flees to the ferry. Arthur Sellman, who has wasted the afternoon dozing at his club after a heavy meal and rounds of liquor, goes to the scene of the riot but is frightened away and also decides to return home by the ferry. Recovering, Lady Hegarty likewise makes her way to the Quay. The fated group is now gathering for what the reader suspects will be a harbor tragedy.

"The Ferry," title of Part IV, opens with the arrival of Lois and the three children at the Sydney Cove wharf. Channon and Sellman chat briefly in the smoking compartment below, but the children and Lady Hegarty enjoy the view from the top deck.

The tragedy strikes. An approaching ocean steamer hits the ferry's stern. The ferry keels over and is cloven in half by the liner's speeding bow. Sirens scream, steam boils the water in which the passengers find themselves struggling, and the harbor is filled with dangerous floating debris and flying objects.

The accident is the crisis of the novel but not the climax, which comes near the end of the final section, Part V, "The Sunset." Then, at the close of his busy day, Oliver Denning sums up the meaning of the events as he observes, *da capo*, the evening view of the harbor, just as he had observed it at sunrise in the opening pages of the book. His life had been interwoven, in one encounter or another, with all the principal members of this suburban cast. The waterway, and the land surrounding it, he concludes, are stronger than any generation of men, and in time will shape humanity to an end in which, optimistically, there will be no conflict between struggling humankind and its environment.

Several reviewers have commented, concerning the plots of this and other Dark novels, that disasters are introduced to solve the problems of individuals, and that this use of the *deus ex machina* is a sign of weakness. Professor Wilkes says of this period: "Both *Sun Across the Sky* and *Waterway* magnify a defect glimpsed earlier: the practice of stating a problem in personal terms, allowing it to develop on its own logic up to a point, and then resolving it by the intervention of some extraneous circumstance. . . . The use of the fire in *Sun Across the Sky* is less convincing still."[2] It should be recalled, though, that the fire was an act of arson motivated by the greed of Gormley, rather than anything extraneous. Regarding *Waterway*, Wilkes declares that "the habit becomes patent artifice."

Both problems posited here — Lesley's dilemma in choosing between Sim and Roger, and Winifred's love for Harnett, thwarted by her marriage to Arthur Sellman — are resolved in this peremptory fashion. Lesley's difficulties are met by the disturbance following the unemployed meeting in the Domain; instead of thinking her problem out in the terms in which it is posed, Lesley makes an intuitive decision for Blair in the stress of the moment. Then the ferry disaster frees Winifred from her impasse. Taking a count of the characters afterward, we discover that Winifred and Harnett were delayed and missed the boat, that the children caught it but have been rescued, that Lois providentially fell asleep on the wharf — and that providence has been singularly unregardful of Arthur. The inconvenient character is thus dispatched from the novel by conveyor-belt; the sympathetic characters are preserved almost intact.[3]

This quotation fails to mention that admirable characters like Professor Channon and Lady Hegarty are also lost in the tragedy, and that Jack Saunders saves himself by his unaided strength. Jack, moreover, rescues Arthur; in the end it is the failure of medical aid on land that results in this timely — but far from regrettable — demise of the most despicable character in the group.[4] A count shows that only a minority of the "main characters" are on the doomed ferry, and only two are lost in the water. This is far from the count in recent "disaster novels," in which an entire cast is often lost together in a holocaust.

The crisis of the ferry accident is based on an actual event.[5] The use of real-life incidents, of course, has resulted in much bad fiction, and the fact that an episode happened to have happened in that precise way does not justify an author in demanding the event's acceptance as a plausible outcome of the fictional situation. Yet we must allow a writer to choose some dramatic plot-event to bring matters to a head, and a ferry disaster is far from a trite selection. It is, in fact, exactly in key with the main setting of the book — Sydney Harbour. Perhaps the final words are found in a *Bulletin* article: "Accidents, which have a way of happening pointlessly, are awkward material for art. . . . Eleanor Dark's accident comes more smoothly into her story . . . clearly a parallel to the *Greycliffe* disaster. . . . Still, such as he is, Arthur does come to his climax in the ferry accident, and so do all the characters and all the situations. And thus, though the accident is not integrally related to the people's lives (as it would be, say, to the crew and officers of the two ships), it is 'near enough.' The accident has, moreover, a certain mystical inevitability . . . the violence immanent in the Australian earth."[6]

Characterization in *Waterway* is, on the whole, more extensive and more convincing than in the earlier novels. The various persons are not sharply divided into "good" and "bad," for this novel is no morality drama. For instance, Arthur Sellman was once attractive enough to become Winifred's husband. In some ways he is as capitalistic as Sir Frederick Gormley in *Sun Across the Sky*, but Arthur's pride and conservatism are better motivated. He is not evil, but stupid. "She [Winifred] thought, with a little shiver, that Nature exacted payment for stupidity, as ruthlessly as for deliberate viciousness. . . . Arthur lived in a kind of half-world — a world from which all but the obvious, the trite, the conventional, was excluded. Among concepts which, for her, for Ian, for all the people she cared about, gave life graciousness and meaning, he blundered like a blind man, irritated, uncomprehending, incredulous" (25 - 26). Moreover, the folk who represent art and culture have human defects; whereas Sim Hegarty is a likable playboy who deserves a better fate than marriage to Lorna, Roger Blair is improvident and irritating in ways that damage his cause. Nor do all the "good" people escape death in the accident; Professor Channon dies when, with six months more to live, he could complete a book of philosophy that might affect civilization.

Channon is the type of radical thinker who lives a bohemian life,

as did Kavanagh in *Sun Across the Sky*. The professor strolls around
the city "in grey flannel trousers and a tweed coat, his round
wrinkled face burnt as dark as a native's under his shock of white
hair, a newspaper parcel under one arm and a couple of books under
the other — and such books!" thinks Lorna. Ironically, both his
daughters, reared in an intellectual household, have chosen wealthy
men whose materialism revolts them.

Winifred, the elder, now a thirty-year-old matron, is inevitably
alienated from Arthur and attracted by the widower Harnett, who
lives next door at the Cove. They have never yielded to their intense
passion, but signal to each other by putting significant objects on
their windowsills. Winifred's maternal instincts are expended not
only upon her blind daughter Brenda but upon the charming
Harnett boys, Brenda's playmates. Winifred's ache for Ian and his
corresponding pain drive them on this critical day into each other's
arms, but when they learn of the ferry disaster, each momentarily
blames the other. " 'Because of you,' their eyes said to each other, 'I
am here and not where I should be' " (396).

The younger daughter, Lesley, aged twenty-three, furnishes the
romantic interest, but her choice of the Socialist editor Blair is made
rather early, and although she had yielded the previous night to Sim
Hegarty, one is well prepared for her refusal to accept the easy and
secure life he can offer. Earlier, Roger tells her: "It may be possible
to adjust a marriage to fit your conception of life, but it's utterly impossible to alter your conception of life to fit your marriage" (233).
And Roger says later, during his casual proposal: "What are you going to do with your spare time, then, if you marry Sim? Read books
that he doesn't read, make friends he doesn't like, think thoughts he
doesn't share, make plans for your children that he doesn't agree
with? . . . Of course you're fond of Sim. . . . But that's not marriage"
(293). Lesley and Sim are parallel lines than can never meet.

To one interested in the author as well as the character, Lesley's
main attraction lies in her resemblance to the young Eleanor
O'Reilly, reared in an intellectual household. Lesley had been born
on August 4, 1914 — date when the British declared war on Germany — and because of this coincidence had concerned herself with
problems of world peace and international amity.[7] She was used to
theory and speculation. "She had been brought up on them. Her
earliest recollections were of lively debates between her father and
any one of a dozen friends who haunted their home to talk to him.
She thought, with a faint bitterness, 'Fathers with a gift for conversa-

tion lay up a peck of trouble for their children!' Ideas, and the words to express them, had been toys of her childhood along with blocks and dolls'' (217).

Brought up, too, in a family where the daughter might have to take more than a share in the household duties, Eleanor as well as Lesley might resent the assumption that these chores are the natural lot of all women. "Father and I like to think we're sensible people. In theory he has his work and I have mine, but automatically, just because I happen to be a female, I become the housekeeper" (102). Again, she reflects, "Ninety-nine women out of a hundred hadn't been trained for domestic work, but they did it all the same" (103). A profound interest in the right of women to have careers might be expected of a daughter with talent and yet with a concern for a happy household. (Lois, the artist wife, is markedly incapable of managing a home.)

Lesley's career, in which she has much facility, is writing. Oliver recalls her "half-contemptuous efficiency" in free-lance journalism (15). Sitting in the Library of New South Wales, scribbling a story of Sydney pioneers,

she knew all the same as she wrote that it would be just another example of deft literary architecture, another neatly-fitting mosaic of words. . . . She had taken to writing stories with this 'period' background several years ago. They had sold well, and that had seemed a sufficient reason for exploiting the vein until it ran out. . . . Armed with a natural perseverance and a dozen pen-names, she scattered through the weekly and monthly journals stories, paragraphs at whose fatuity she scowled or giggled according to her mood, brief articles, household hints, gardening hints, dressmaking hints and even, upon occasion, when she felt impish, mothercraft hints. . . . She had a flair, too, for innocuous verse. . . . (217 - 19)

Roger had disdained the stories and said that she "had the critical, not the creative mind." He implied that she should do something more intellectual than merely turn out fiction. It is needful to the novel that Lesley have a suitable occupation, and literature fits well. None the less, the choice of this vocation says much about Eleanor Dark and her feeling that novels should hold ideas as well as events.

*Waterway* has a number of characters who are sketched in greater or less detail. Even the servants, shop assistants, and Bobby Younger, a boy on the ferry, receive more attention than the minimum. The children are charming. Lorna Sellman is the type of hollow flapper who has nothing but loveliness, and that is fading. Chloe Marshall, Denning's stepdaughter, does not seem to have a plot role, but is merely inherited from *Sun Across the Sky*. Lady Hegarty, schoolmaster's daughter who had married a merchant and had gotten used to being rich, is "fat, clumsy, elderly, weary" (57) but "only today, for some strange reason, life had become intense again." On the birthday of her son Sim, she reaches an awareness that is to be brutally cut short.

Roger Blair, who wins over Sim in courtship, is fourteen years older than Lesley, and her future with him will be uncertain but exciting. "His fair skin, refusing tan, had settled down long ago to a fierce brick red, against which his short moustache showed tow-colored and his eyes a brilliant and imperative blue. . . . It was his nature at all times to do as many things at once as was humanly possible" (85). The reader is told further that not taking the easy path "was merely a result, logical if trifling, of an inherent faculty for combat, a chemical peculiarity of cell tissue, perhaps, which endowed him with an inexhaustible energy and resilience" (86). He is, apparently, the lone champion in philistine Australia of the need for a national culture, a chance to build a country free from the festering diseases of Europe's senility.[8]

Jack Saunders — born on the same day as Sim Hegarty, but without a silver spoon in his mouth — is meant to symbolize the willing unemployed who stood in dole lines during the 1930s in Australia as well as in other countries. He is proud of his strength and independence, which are disdained by city people, and his anger finds an outlet in violence. At the end of the book, assured that he is not a murderer, he decides to go "up country" and seek to put to use the physical powers that are not wanted on the wharves of Sydney. His admiration for Oliver, whose surgery he enters to get his injured hand treated, is based chiefly on the fact that the doctor has a job to do and does it skillfully.

Far from being minor characters, the Dennings, who were the most important ones in *Sun Across the Sky*, are also highly central to the figures who people *Waterway*. This book begins and ends with reveries by Oliver. His position as a suburban medico enables him to meet and assay almost all of the cast. Again, this choice of a leading character is more than a reflection of Mrs. Dark's life as a doctor's wife. Oliver is the objective scientist, whose judgment we respect but whose compassion we value even more highly. He is married to his opposite, Lois, the artist — a creature moved strongly by instinctive rightness wedded to inborn powers of observation and technique. Still searching to express most fully her genius, she is careless of convention and household affairs, but her unfeigned naturalness charms her husband and creates an atmosphere of peace. To assume that Lesley's romance is the high point of this novel is to overlook the subtle but emergent strength of the Dennings' marriage and their influence on their neighbors at Watson's Bay.

The setting of *Waterway* is of equal importance to the characterization. It is not only suburban but urban, with scenes of the Quay, the library, the Domain, Macquarie Place, St. James' Church, and a gentleman's club. The harbor, however, is the dominant scene, which becomes almost a symbol. This waterway is mentioned in the opening line of the novel, and recurs thereafter. Its flat expanse — fifteen miles long, interspersed with islands and headlands, ships and yachts, overarched by a massive bridge, marked by the wakes of ferries plying to Manly and Hunters Hill, bright with gulls — is viewed by various characters at different hours of the day. What other novel gives such a loving portrait of Sydney and its sprawling harbor?

Ian Harnett, who is appropriately an official of the Port of Sydney, stands on South Head at the narrow space between the harbor beach and the cliff where the ill-fated *Dunbar* had driven into The Gap. "He turned his back on the ocean and looked up the harbor, dull silver like a misted blade in this early light, winding and threading westward till it became lost in a vaporous nothingness, partly sky, partly distance; and for the first time he thought of it as the main highway of the city" (40). The smell of salt water is in the nostrils of the people as they move about on shore, and their chief conveyance to the city is not the winding roadway but the ferry, plying from wharf to wharf. Lesley thinks of the changeless harbor: "It was so vitally a part of the city, so entangled in one way or another with the lives of its inhabitants, in so true a sense their highway and their playground, that its permanence seemed to promise them, too, security and anchorage" (218).

The ending of the book shows Oliver watching the sunset. "The long waterway beneath lost itself in a western haze of paling gold, the bridge spanned it like a rainbow, the city skyline sank into a lavender-colored mist. . . . A little sailing-boat with all her canvas out was racing for the Heads, making for the harbor like a bird homing" (445). Such lyric passages are scattered through the novel, to unite the movements of its people against a shining background.

The use of setting is strengthened by quotations at the beginning of each part — lines from early descriptions of the harbor ranging from 1788 to 1863. *Waterway* misses being "atmosphere" fiction, however, because the harbor setting, although it is important and the scene of the crisis, has no strong, impelling effect upon the actions of the characters.

The method used in *Waterway* is again the interior monologue. It is used not out of weary habit but because, once more, Eleanor Dark feels that this is the best way for her to tell her story. She is interested not only in what happens but why it happens, and human actions are seldom instinctive — they are usually preceded by thought if not by logic. In Part I, we learn that Oliver "had always enjoyed those idle meanderings of thought which supplemented so royally the pleasure of mere logical reasoning, so that the mind became a thing mysterious and infinite, retreating but never altering, as a reflected figure retreats down an endless succession of mirrors" (50). This reflective habit may lose the name of action. Channon tells himself: "Once, perhaps, we knew how to . . . remain quietly just living, just glorying in life. But now we can only think, and think our thoughts, and think of our thoughts of our thoughts, until we go so deep into the mystery and darkness of our minds that we see the lunatic hidden in each one of us peering back into our fearful eyes. For the delights of intricate thinking, of making patterns with ideas, of building words and forms and sounds into triumphant structures, of playing Peeping Tom to our own wild hearts, that is the risk we have to face, and the penalty we sometimes have to pay" (140). A mind observing its mind may become a sort of mental narcissism.

Throughout the course of this critical day, from sunrise to sunset, we share in the "meanderings" of the minds of more than a dozen citizens of Sydney. The transitions are usually smooth, and at times the shifts from one mind to another, as the characters move about the city, recall the earlier use of the same technique in the "Wandering Rocks" episode in James Joyce's *Ulysses*.

*Waterway* received little attention in Australia when it was published in London and New York in 1938. One notice considered it "merely an extension of the outlook and technique employed in its predecessor, *Sun Across the Sky*. . . . A harbor disaster is made the climax of the book. It is here, unfortunately, that the scaffolding becomes most obvious — the author rather too omnipotent. . . . She expresses herself in good and fluent prose, and those who are interested in the development of Australian fiction cannot afford to miss her book."[9]

American reviewers were more enthusiastic. Percy Hutchinson remarked that "it would be a joy to read it for its literary excellence alone. . . . This strict adherence to a definite technique has not, however, lessened Miss Dark's vital interest in people. . . . She does not argue or take sides. . . . *Waterway* will more than satisfy the fundamental demand for fiction, which is that it be neither too light nor too heavy and shall be done in the best novel tradition."[10] George Dangerfield said: "Miss Dark has not quite succeeded in distinguishing between wilderness and labyrinth, between multiplicity of characters and interaction of characters. . . . But, as you read it, it does seem as if an infinitesimal part of the map of the world had suddenly shivered and come alive; and to have achieved this is, in itself, success."[11] Mona Harrop declared that "here is a thoroughly satisfying novel, one which tells a story competently, reveals character, captures the attention, and provokes the reader to thoughtfulness."[12]

Attention was again directed to the novel when it was reprinted in Sydney in 1946. A lengthy review stated that "actually, when you review the thin ranks of our living, worthwhile writers, you find it hard to find one who has produced a book comparable in all respects to *Waterway*. . . . The importance of this book and of Eleanor Dark's work in general is that it is civilized. This woman is more than an accomplished storyteller; she is a cultured and highly intelligent person who puts into her novels not only a sometimes uncanny understanding of human nature, but her own philosophy of living. . . . *Waterway* is one of the few novels in which an attempt has been made to examine and reproduce in fiction the pattern of contemporary Australian urban life."[13]

Little attention has been paid to this long novel by serious critics since publication of the first edition. The following commentators give no judgments on *Waterway:* Eric Lowe (1951), Harry Heseltine (1964), T. Inglis Moore (1971), and Humphrey McQueen (1971). Cecil Hadgraft in a 1960 book merely remarks: "In *Waterway* (1938) the manner of telling has grown into a mannerism. A tendency observable before is here manifest, a slightly hortatory note: the author is beginning to preach a little, not about politics, but about life, which is shown as real and earnest."[14] The 1950 comment by G. A. Wilkes, previously mentioned, is rather unfavorable. Perhaps the most solid consideration is that by Colin Roderick in the same year, including such sentences as: "And how well conceived and skilfully contrasted these characters are! . . . Sunlight and shadow occur as in life to create an atmosphere that is potent and convincing. . . . Does not such a passage make us realize suddenly that there is a rich field for both romance and realism in the life of our immediate neighborhood?"[15]

The present chapter, it is hoped, should show that of all her ten novels, Eleanor Dark's most underappreciated one is *Waterway*.

## CHAPTER 6

# The Timeless Time

THE sesquicentennial of the settlement of Australia by the First Fleet in 1788 was celebrated in 1938. As part of the commemoration, Eleanor Dark was asked to write an essay on Caroline Chisholm for a memorial volume about women pioneers, which appeared in that year.[1] This research made her more aware of the rich possibilities for fiction in the history of Australia.

Mrs. Dark's thoughts had already turned to producing "period" fiction, as shown by a passage in *Waterway*. The young writer Lesley Channon is sitting in the Library of New South Wales, reading old journals and histories and dreaming of the first colonists in Sydney Cove.

An inhospitable land, they said; a barren, hostile country. . . . Hostile — no. It had never descended far enough from its majestic aloofness to be hostile. There it was, here it is still, untouched. Not it, she thought, but we, its invaders, have changed. . . . She had begun to suspect that her tenacious use of this period as a setting for her tales might have its roots in her own limitations. A careful attention to historical facts, an accuracy of historical detail — these were matters rightly into her hands; and if the stories had a dim unreality, a decorative air as of a formal design, perhaps it seemed not altogether unnatural in stories of a time and place so unfamiliar to their readers?[2]

The writing of historical fiction was to occupy Mrs. Dark for the next fifteen years, resulting in the celebrated trilogy beginning with *The Timeless Land,* published in 1941. This book was written between September, 1937, and July, 1940 — years during which another world war erupted because of European materialism — and even an historical motif in a novel could not fail to be affected by the events of that fateful period.

The genesis of the series and the author's doubts about its success were revealed to an interviewer. "I was reading up a lot of early historical material and scattered throughout many books I found allusions to the man Bennilong. From them all the personality of the man gradually emerged and gripped me. He became a living person to me. So much so that I collected all the items and began to weave a story around him. And I couldn't write about Bennilong without writing about his environment, and so the book took shape. What I liked best about it? Finishing it! I was very dubious about it. Every book is bad compared with the mental picture one starts out with and *The Timeless Land* was no exception."[3]

The genre of historical fiction requires the writer to decide whether he will sacrifice history to fiction or fiction to history, for seldom do actual events shape themselves in a sequence that is a ready-made scenario for a work of art. Mrs. Dark chose to follow historical fidelity, but none the less her sense of story did not fail her, because she selected from the multiplicity of events those which well served her theme, and her abiding interest in people enlivened the pages. Although her extensive researches in aboriginal culture and the founding of Sydney enabled her to retain authenticity, she molded them into a narrative which avoids being a mere collection of annals.[4] This she did by using her sharpened instrument, the interior monologue; most of the narrative consists of a series of reveries by various characters.

## I  *"Indians" Lurking in the "Woods"*

The authenticity of *The Timeless Land* was so effective that in her preface to the 1965 edition Mrs. Dark added these opening words: "This book has borrowed so much from history that it seems advisable to remind readers that it is fiction" (9).[5] The preface continues with the statement that the author's aim "has been to give a picture of the first settlement of Sydney, which is always true in broad outline, and often in detail, but I make no claim to strict historical accuracy either in my dealings with the white men or the black." The point is, however, that authenticity in this book is secondary. Its primary contribution is story — a parable of the universal conflict between tribal and "civilized" society. In this classic novel Mrs. Dark shows her social conscience at its most sensitive — so sensitive that many critics have overlooked its barbed commentary on twentieth-century morality.

Also in the preface the author strongly reveals her main theme in a statement that no critic could rival. "I do not want to be taken for a 'back-to-nature' advocate, nor for one who, in these disillusioned times, regards our own civilization as inevitably doomed; but I do believe that we, nine-tenths of whose 'progress' has been a mere elaboration and improvement of the technique, as opposed to the art of living, might have learned much from a people who, whatever they may have lacked in technique, had developed that art to a very high degree. 'Life, liberty, and the pursuit of happiness' — to us a wistful phrase, describing a far-away goal — sums up what was, to them, a taken-for-granted condition of their existence" (10).

The book shows again and again that men do not conquer a land. The land conquers men. To try to possess a continent by raising a flagpole and reading a commission is, as Governor Arthur Phillip realizes, a ridiculous gesture. Men must adapt to their environment, and in the process of adapting to the upside-down ecosystem of Port Jackson, the "invaders" will destroy a balanced culture that had taken thousands of years to develop. Time — time is the key to adaptation, and the words "time" and "land" appear virtually on every page of the novel. To be able to adapt, one must have freedom — another key word. The aborigines are free souls, who lose their freedom when they are driven from their land and their waterways. They suffer from the exploitation of property-minded people like the capitalist-emigrant Stephen Mannion.

The tribes of the Port Jackson region are portrayed as happily living a communal existence. An individual could own a few personal items — a shield, a spear, a canoe — but the land and its produce could not belong to any one person. Captain Watkin Tench utters a revolutionary thought "whose obvious common sense was, even a century and a half later, to remain unappreciated" when he wrote in his journal: "But toil cannot be long supported without adequate refreshment. The first step in any community which wishes to preserve honesty, should be to set the people above want" (290 - 91). In this respect the convicts — many of whom were guilty of no crime except poverty — were in the same plight as the dispossessed natives, whose Law was opposed to that of bourgeois Europe: "Property must remain sacred or the whole elaborate structure of the white man's world, its complicated social and economic system, its highly adaptable code of ethics, its triumphant culture, must collapse" (291).

The failure of the aborigines lies in their inability to fathom the European mind. "It was a mind which had gained subtlety and lost simplicity, a mind which explored the universe, but had long, long ago lost sight of itself. It was a mind which, finding its activities incompatible with its faith, had gradually substituted for that faith a system of mechanical worship by which it was enabled to believe that it might simultaneously serve God and Mammon. It was a mind which had become so active, so ingenious, so tough, so flexible, so tortuous, that it was able to make a show of holding apart the indivisible forces of man's soul" (110). Again, the flaws in the imperialistic civilization of George III are clearly in Bennilong's thoughts at the end of the book.

> They had been the means whereby he had fulfilled his destiny, and journeyed across the sea to a land which no man of his race had seen before. But he despised them. They were not good hunters; they could not see tracks upon the ground, be they clear as day. There was no valor in their fighting; they never fought as men fight, hand to hand, strength matched with strength, but stood afar off, and killed by magic. They were squeamish, expressing horror and repugnance at certain tribal customs, and yet they held many of their own race to infamous subjection and inflicted upon them indignities which turned the black men cold with loathing.
> They had not one Law, but two, and disobeyed them both. . . . (397)

From the point of view of the aborigines, the invaders were both materialistic and hypocritical.

Time will modify the actions of the newcomers to suit the rigors of the land. Governor Phillip muses on time: "On his little journey from the cradle to the grave, how comforting to feel that Time moved forward with him — how chilling, how strange, how awesome, to feel, as one felt here, that Time was static, a vast, eternal unmoving emptiness through which the tiny pathway of one's life ran from darkness into darkness and was lost. It was the silence he thought that stretched one's nerves. A man should feel about him the stir of his own restless spirit, he should see the fruits of his energy and his inventiveness, he should hear the sounds of his multifarious activities" (43). Even the children of England are work-oriented. Johnny Prentice, four-year-old convict lad, wanders to a native camp and spends the afternoon pouring water from one gum-tree cup to another, while the black children flit about him like idle butterflies (72).

Discussing the main intention of this novel, a recent critic, who feels that "in the stress of fear during the second world war *The Timeless Land* was misread as a justification of European settlement when it was, in fact, a scarifying assault on the Australia of the 1930s, torn as it was with the ravages of economic depression and class war-

fare," added, concerning Mrs. Dark: "Her attachment to the countryside and her fond hopes for its inhabitants cannot add up to
political nationalism. Civilization stands as a barrier between her
love of Australia as a natural phenomenon and her rejection of
Australia as a socio-political manifestation; a barrier between her
patriotism and her nationalism. Clearly she did not despair of their
reconciliation, and her novels are partly intended to awaken
Australians to the task of an entirely new kind of nation-building.
There is little indication of how this is to be achieved on a political
level. However, the creative artist has a special power."[6]

The action of *The Timeless Land* follows chronology and deals
chiefly with the first five years of the settlement of Sydney colony.
The story is not a chronicle, however; Mrs. Dark selects rigidly the
events that enforce her theme. This can be shown by comparing Part
I of the novel, say, with a day-to-day account drawn from contemporary records.[7] She omits mention of a number of various episodes
which do not reveal character or advance the action.

To give a complete synopsis of the events narrated would be
tedious and might dull the enjoyment of the unfolding story about
the founding of an important Pacific commonwealth. Some mention
of main events, however, will help to explain the theme and il-
luminate the characters.

What is the main conflict in this novel? A shrewd critic has termed
the book

one of the most convincing accounts we have in our literature of the clash of
cultures, of the tragedies and frustrations which involved both the
goodwilled men of enlightenment on the one side and the "Indians" lurking
in the "woods" on the other, as they tried to establish some kind of contact
of mind. Earthmen might as well try to live in a methane atmosphere as for
the European colonizers, however well-intentioned, to come to any intellectual terms with the aboriginals. . . . In *The Timeless Land* the conflict is personified in the two essentially generous and gentle natures of Governor
Phillip and Bennilong, and the novel is sustained by the tautness of the interplay, not only between these two protagonists and the groups they represent, but also by the feeling we are given that, while both men represent
their own groups, yet they also stand apart from, and to some extent in antagonism to, their own background.[8]

## II   *Tragedy for the Tribes*

Bennilong is the character to whom the events mean the most, and
the novel opens and closes with transcriptions of his thoughts. At the
age of six, he is taken to South Head by his father, Wunbula, song-

maker and artist of the tribe, to look out to sea for the return of the winged boat that had passed along the coast in 1770 (the bark *Endeavour*, captained by James Cook, discoverer of eastern Australia, on the first of his three epochal voyages in the Pacific). Part I, longest section of the book, covers the period from Bennilong's childhood to the end of the year 1788. Inspired, Wunbula knows that the destiny of Bennilong is linked with the image of the magic boat that he chips on a rock.

The invaders make their first contact with the natives at Botany Bay, but the First Fleet, consisting of eleven ships conveying convicts and their guards from England, soon moves to Sydney Cove, in the spreading harbor of Port Jackson. Tents are set up ashore, and the convicts are disembarked, including women and children, guarded by the corps of Marines. A flag is raised and men begin to clear away the trees and erect crude shelters. Frightening weather, death by native spears, quarrels between the civil and military arms of the minuscule colony, thefts by both blacks and whites, and starvation rations mark the months to the end of the first painful year. Bennilong and his wife, Barangaroo, observe the strange actions of the newcomers from afar, for their friend Arabanoo has been captured and, instead of being killed as an enemy, is kept manacled, to be studied by the governor and his men. Ellen Prentice and her Johnny are reunited with Andrew, father of the convict family, but Andrew plots to win to freedom, and on the last day of the year escapes into the fastnesses of the west. Governor Phillip patiently ponders the future, looks toward the beckoning blue hills inland, and does not regret his writing to Lord Sydney the words "nor do I doubt that this country will prove the most valuable acquisition Great Britain ever made."

In Part II, covering the year 1789, relations with the natives are further strained by a smallpox epidemic which carries off, among others, the patient captive Arabanoo. Prentice survives among the inland tribes and a woman, Cunnembeillee, is given to him to help haul his precious stolen possessions, with which property he feels more secure. Bennilong is very ill, and his tribe is scattered. A settlement is made at Rose Hill, at the west end of the harbor, and from it exploring parties set out, but are baffled by the roughness of the land.

The year 1790, dealt with in Part III, is marked by Andrew Prentice's discovery that the cattle that had wandered away from Sydney Cove had survived and thrived. He adds the herd to his growing estate and works daily to build a house and a yard for the cattle. The settlement's supply ship *Sirius* is wrecked on Norfolk Island, where an agricultural colony had been set up by Lieutenant King. The exiles have passed three years at Sydney Cove without a word from the home country; the land holds them as in a vise, helpless and starving. In June the *Lady Juliana*, forerunner of the Second Fleet of convicts, arrives with the first family of free settlers — Stephen Mannion, his invalid wife Harriet, and a six-year-old son, Patrick. The Second Fleet arrives, laden with convicts that did not die on the voyage, and these swell the numbers of useless folk to be fed and sheltered. Through a misunderstanding with the natives, Governor Phillip is speared in the right shoulder, adding this wound to the chronic pain in his side. The Parramatta district at the head of the harbor is developed by the first farmers. Bennilong, as interpreter, becomes a welcome visitor at the governor's house, despite his quarrelsomeness. An attempt at a punitive expedition, seeking to capture a native accused of murder, ends ignominiously; the quarry simply disappears into the forest.

In Part IV, covering the year 1791, Andrew Prentice's hideout is threatened by exploring parties, and he decides to move farther westward — a forerunner of the great movements to follow. The class system imported from England begins to break down; as Phillip muses: "This little world which he had founded and governed was too small; discomfort, exile, hunger and despair had welded into one community two classes which in their own country had been the poles apart"; (310). But Mannion, an aristocrat, begins to set up an estate, with convict labor, inland beyond Parramatta. The Marines under Major Ross depart, to be replaced by the New South Wales Corps, a body of volunteers that was to gain supreme power in the colony in the next few years.

The final year covered in the novel, 1792, is the frame for Part V. Prentice has become a virtual member of the aboriginal folk, and his homestead is safely moved beyond the influence of the colonists. Bennilong acquires a second wife, a young woman to help the failing Barangaroo, who is suckling the girl child Dilboong. Governor Phillip is not satisified with Mannion's view of the future of the colony, and warns him: "You intend to exploit this land. Have a care, sir, that it does not end by exploiting you!" (340). Prentice sacrifices his hard-earned freedom to save his black wife and their child from a flash flood, and his young son Johnny inherits the secret farmstead. Phillip prepares to lay down his five-year burden and sail for England, leaving Major Grose of the New South Wales Corps in charge. Phillip foresees the war between the settlers and the implacable land: "He saw them, driven by their reckless greed, and by an obscure urge for conquest of so aloof and invulnerable a foe, exhausting her earth, fouling her rivers, despoiling her trees, savagely imposing upon the pattern of her native loveliness traditional forms which meant beauty in other lands. He heard them crying out to her insatiably: 'Give! Give!' and was aware of her silent inviolability which would never give until they had ceased to rob" (370). Accompanied by Bennilong and young Immerawanye, he sails in the *Atlantic*, never to return.

The brief "Epilogue" shows Bennilong, returning with the new governor, John Hunter, after three years amid the rains and snows of England, unable to resume his tribal mores. Hunter and Collins discuss the plight of the colony, in which the military had subverted civil rule, and they foresee the problems that will be dealt with in the sequel volume, *Storm of Time*. Penetration of the inland is impeded by the ruggedness of the countryside; opening up the rich interior must await the arduous adventures to be related in the third volume of the trilogy, *No Barrier*. Coming full circle to the headland where, at the age of six, Bennilong had watched with his father for the coming of the white invaders, the dispossessed native can look forward to nothing but despair and the consolations of rum. His vision of loveliness has been replaced by "an exhausting and unendurable sense of loss." Thus the action of *The Timeless Land* declines into passive gloom and defeat.

The principal virtue of this first of the historical series, according to Colin Roderick, is "that it is as good a representation as we are ever likely to have of the unique character of the birth of the Australian nation." [9] It is indeed unlikely that any other writer will have the skill — and the patience — to retell this great story in fictional guise.

Characterization in *The Timeless Land* shows Eleanor Dark at her most skillful best in handling a number of actors who individualize themselves through their attitudes as revealed in their thoughts. One critic felt that the book "contains so many characters that interest is diffused," [10] but a listing of those who are presented in some detail is not so long as to discourage analysis.

Among the aboriginals, Bennilong is given the most treatment in depth. He, like most of the others in the cast, was a real person; Bennelong Point, site of the celebrated Sydney Opera House, was named for him, and there he had his home. His qualities are not un-attractive: his skill in hunting, his sudden, passing rages, his vanity, lightheartedness, buffoonery and mimicry, skill in making songs, joy in freedom — "a lonely, comic, tragic, and immortal figure" (39). "His mind was the mind of his race — quick, subtle, eager, volatile" (95). He is a "revolutionary" among the tribesmen, willing to frater-nize with the invaders. Bennilong is the romantic, as Phillip is the realist; Bennilong is the artist, as Phillip is the administrator. Ben-nilong develops from a carefree boy to a man who has spent three years in England, has met King George, and has learned only the vices of "civilized" existence. The apparently friendly newcomers are his subtle enemies. His life comes *da capo* when he returns, with a bottle of rum in his hand, to the spot where, at the age of six, he had seen his father carve on a rock the image of Captain Cook's ex-ploring ship. Now, in 1795, he has lost his wife and fought with Colbee, who represents the finest leadership in the tribe. Bennilong is not fully accepted, on the other hand, by the Europeans, who ridicule him and find him a troublemaker. He is neither all black nor all white. He has lost the eternity of the "dream time" and entered the tyranny of the clock. His crisis is the culmination of the novel.

He had lost that close and serene communion with mystery, by which the inner life of his people was nourished and sustained. Once, he thought, life was whole, like the body of a man. Once the past, the present, and the future were intricately woven together, and with them was entwined the life of man, body and spirit, one life. . . . But now something had assailed it. Change had gashed it like a knife, and the spirit flowed out of it like blood. There had been betrayal — but where was the betrayer? There was an enemy — but what was his name? There was no single man, white or black, to whom he could point in his fury of despair. The very earth had played him false, showing him a land of grey skies and naked trees, and the heavens had deceived him with unfamiliar stars. But worse, he thought, far worse than all, mankind itself had betrayed him (398 - 99).

Bennilong has "forgotton how to be at peace." The swift twilight of his land creeps about him to cover his defeat. The story is a tragedy, for the protagonist and his tribe are overwhelmed by insuperable odds, as all the other tribes of the continent were to be overwhelmed.

### III  *Determined to Become "Gentry"*

Aside from Wunbula the song-maker and Colbee the leader, the male aborigines who are memorable are few. Most prominent is

Arabanoo, another real person. He is a gentle soul who loves to play with children and who is patient in captivity. Balledery is a native whose canoe has been damaged; he is man enough to take personal action against the white wrongdoer, but cannot understand how the governor could be satisfied with secondhand reprisal, by ordering a flogging of the culprits. Immerawanye is the lad who accompanies Bennilong to England and dies there, far from his homeland.

Eleanor Dark's interest in feminism is strongly shown in her presentation of aboriginal women. Carangarang and Warreweer are Bennilong's sisters; the former is domestic, the latter a wayward maiden and song-maker. Barangaroo, Bennilong's shrewish wife, is given a compelling personality, as is Cunnembeillie, Andrew Prentice's native wife. Gooroobarooboolo is Bennilong's comely young second wife, who forsakes him at the end. Daringha is the wife of the noble Colbee. Aboriginal children include Nanbarree and Boo-ron, who spend some months in the white camp; Billalong or "Bill," son of Prentice and Cunnembeillee, representing the early mingling of the two races; and Dilboong, daughter of Bennilong and Barangaroo, born in 1791. "What was to be the fate of Dilboong in the land which was hers no longer?" (318).

Concerning the faithfulness of characterization of the native people in the novel, an Australian critic has remarked, *ex cathedra:* "Thoughts are assigned to the natives of which they could never have been aware, and the treatment is sentimental. All the qualities of meanness and treachery in the settlement belong exclusively to the whites; the aborigines live in guileless innocence."[11] This is hardly true. Most of the original officers of Sydney Cove, especially the high-minded Phillip, are decent human beings, and the natives have weaknesses that make them vulnerable. Another critic has stated, with more truth: "*The Timeless Land* was almost certain to be misinterpreted. It was precisely in the alleged over-sophistication of the aboriginal mind, and the resulting imposition of an alien type of life upon the habits and customs and rhythm of thought of a primitive stone-age people that the technique of the deeper theme was to be found. Looked at superficially, the objection that it is an unreal presentation of the aboriginal mind and thought may be admitted, but apart from the narrative itself, the author herself says, 'I must emphatically insist that my portrayal is not intended to be taken too literally.' "[12] This critic concludes: "Other Australian writers have juxtaposed the aboriginal with the white man with more formal scientific truth, but not with the depth of insight, imagination, and range Eleanor Dark has shown."[13] This is indeed a deserved laudation.

The treatment of the aboriginal race by Europeans through two centuries should by this time be well understood. As one Australian writer recently said: "What is needed is an exact and detailed teaching in the schools of the horrors the aborigines suffered as a result of the British seizure of their lands. In Sydney and the other capital cities there should be statues in expiation of these atrocities."[14] The continued teaching of *The Timeless Land* in the schools would well serve this effort at expiation.

Captain Arthur Phillip, R.N. is the leader and representative of the British plan to deport to "Botany Bay" the dregs of English prisons and hulks. He arrives as the wise commodore of the famed First Fleet, and for the first five years of the settlement of New South Wales is the absolute ruler of the Port Jackson region. In the novel, Phillip is revealed as Plato's philosopher-king. This ugly, fifty-year-old little man with the big nose had an inborn will of steel. The author in her preface states: "It is not easy to catch more than a glimpse here and there of Arthur Phillip the man in the voluminous dispatches and correspondence of Arthur Phillip the Governor. The comments of his contemporaries shed a little light — his actions and the results of his actions more still. Certain qualities appear too obviously to be questioned — physical courage and endurance, moral fortitude, a struggling humanitarianism, and a streak of illogical faith. Upon these qualities I have built what must be regarded merely as my own conception of the founder of Australia" (10).

The governor's task is to control not only the convicts but also his own forces and the threatening aborigines. He knows that the settlers must work to survive. "He knew that if he once allowed idleness to grip the community they were all doomed" (302). His conflicts are mainly outward, whereas Bennilong's conflict is within himself — the clash between his inborn conservatism and his desire to learn the ways of the white men. However, Phillip also has an inward dilemma: "Duty pushed him one way, and humanity the other, but it was an unequal contest; he had been bred to revere the former" (272). His humane thoughts were impossible ones for a middle-aged naval captain, molded to the service of king and country. An eminent Australian critic has said that the greater part of *The Timeless Land* might conceivably be regarded as "a widely extended life of Phillip; no other book, of fiction or of history either, has brought us so close to the man but for whom the first settlement of Australia might well have failed."[15]

The plaint that this novel contains too many characters is again unjustified. Among the some eighty officers of the First Fleet, the author chooses less than a dozen for presentation. These are Major Robert Ross, the overbearing lieutenant-governor and officer commanding the Marine Corps, who stands on his dignity and is a nuisance to Phillip until he is sent off to command at Norfolk Island; Captain David Collins, judge advocate as well as secretary to the governor — a quiet and competent subordinate; the Reverend Richard Johnson, chaplain, who is more interested in his garden than in his God; John White, despairing surgeon-general, who is hampered by widespread illness and lack of supplies; Captain John Hunter, master of the ill-fated ship *Sirius;* Lieutenant Phillip Gidley King, aide-de-camp, who is the pioneer settler of Norfolk Island; Lieutenants George Johnston and William Dawes, who were to be explorers of the western outskirts; and Captain Watkin Tench, also of the Marines. Of these, we are closest to the nonchalant Tench, author of a charming early journal. In fact, most of the chosen characters were writers of surviving documents, and selections from their journals add much authenticity to the narrative.[16]

Stephen Mannion, a wealthy Irish gentleman who succumbs to an impulse to emigrate to Australia with his family, is a representative of the capitalist class. He is one of the earliest free settlers of the Hawkesbury region and founder of a colonial family; but he sees in the land only a chance for economic exploitation. He is, however, more than a Gormley or an Arthur Sellman. Mannion has a personality which, although unlikable, is more individualized than those of such type figures. When his wife dies of her hardships, he takes Ellen Prentice as a housekeeper and mistress. He suffers "a complete moral collapse" and his desires sink to an animal level. But he has the means to make his farm a model development, and to enable his son Patrick to become one of the first aristocrats of the new colony.

Few convict characters appear in the book by name, although their lot is dismal and they represent the rejected classes of Europe. For most, there is no hope. But foremost among them is Andrew Prentice, the red-haired, energetic rebel who escapes and sets up a thriving farmstead in the wilderness. Slowly, through the help of the natives, he adapts to the land, and at the crisis earns regeneration by sacrifice. His wife, Ellen, is a contriving climber and mother of three offspring. Their son Johnny is a canny, self-taught user of expediency, who at the end replaces his father as an illegal landowner and feeds his determination to become "gentry" like his playmate Patrick Mannion, through the use of money.

Mrs. Dark's interest in women characters has little scope among the earliest settlers, for only a few white women, like Mrs. Johnson and Mrs. John Macarthur, are residents of Sydney. She therefore puts aboriginal women to use in showing feminine roles in the colony. Moreover, she does mention a brave convict woman, Mary Bryant, whose full story must be sought elsewhere.[17]

## IV Civilization is Implicitly Arraigned

The setting of *The Timeless Land* is the Port Jackson region during the years 1788 to 1793. The area is so convincingly and powerfully presented that some reviewers have claimed that the land is the protagonist.[18] This is, of course, illogical; setting cannot be character. The influence of the environment, however, is the chief motivating force for much of the action. Immediately after landing, the Europeans must begin to modify their habits to fit the demands of the antipodes. The "land" dominates the puny efforts of the invading forces, which slowly but inevitably will be conditioned by geographical factors. In the process the land, too, will suffer.

Eleanor Dark is often at her most poetic in passages that reveal her love of the region — especially the wild stretches of forest and stream that comprise the "bush." The land is personified by its aboriginal inhabitants, who for thousands of years have yielded gracefully to its monitorial pressures. The author's loving depiction of her country provides a moving tapestry, a panorama of scenes and people that for many readers evokes the best vision of early Sydney. One passage, among many that could be selected, shows the melody of her prose:

Here it was as if the pulse of life in plant, and beast, and man had slowed almost to immobility, taking its beat from the land itself, which had all eternity in which to change. Here life was marooned, and Time, like a slowly turning wheel, was only night and day, night and day, summer and winter, birth and death, the ebb and swell of tides. Nothing showed for the passing of the ages but a minutely changing coastline, an infinitesimal wearing away of mountains, a barely discernible lifting of coral reefs. Still the ancient grass-tree thrust its tall spear towards the sky; still the platypus laid its eggs and suckled its young as it had done in primeval times; and still through the

high tops of the gum-trees the blue thread of smoke from the black man's
fire wavered into the uncorrupted air. (19 - 20)

The style of *The Timeless Land* is unified throughout. The
method of reporting thoughts of leading characters is here justified;
this subjective device seems the natural way to narrate the story, and
lends immediacy to old events, colored as they are by individual
feelings. Dialogue avoids the "odds-bodkins" and "unhand-me-sir"
imitations of eighteenth-century vulgate found in popular romances.
Conversations are few but are conducted in standard, somewhat
stilted English. The use of aboriginal words lends a local flavor but is
not overdone; a two-page Glossary of such terms is given, but con-
text usually explains meaning. As H. M. Green so well describes it,
the style in this novel and its sequel "is, as was to be expected, individual, competent, and extremely concise and precise: it is the
style of a scholar who has not been overweighted by his scholarship,
a literary man whom reading has scarcely at all formalized; and this
in spite of the extracts from documents, varyingly formal, with
which the books are interspersed, in spite of their foundation upon
such documents, and in spite of the more formal manners of the time
to which they endeavor to hold up the most accurate of mirrors. It is
a practical style, in that it comes to the point at once and wastes no
words, but at the same time it is sensitive and streaked with
poetry."[19]

*The Timeless Land* appeared in October, 1941, two months before
America entered World War II, and almost two years after Britain
entered the global conflict. There was space, however, for generous
reviews of this book, and reviewers on both sides of the Atlantic at
once recognized that here was a masterpiece.

Klaus Lambrecht noted in the *Saturday Review of Literature:*

Mrs. Dark has gathered her material both from British sources and from a
careful study of all accounts of the tribal life of the aborigines. This enables
her to give — for the first time, I believe — a two-sided view of the settlement in its early stage and makes her judgment an extremely balanced
one. . . . In fact, the inevitable continuity of dreariness and desperation, of
hunger and exhaustion that necessarily accompanies an undertaking so ill-
equipped in every respect, might very well be monotonous, if it were not for
the decided moral growth in the characters whose destinies are shaped by it.
Very rarely in modern literature does one find that persons are so sparingly
described, revealing themselves only in their reactions, and yet are fully
rounded characters who stand out clearly for their truly human qualities. . . .

The result is a novel of stern beauty and profound reality which unquestionably ranks among the best books of the year.[20]

Hassoldt Davis, on the same date in the *Nation*, remarked: "For the first time, I believe, we see in graphic full scale the initial conflicts and adjustments of a dark race with a white one. Largely it is the natives' story here, and Mrs. Dark has so intelligently portrayed them that they are never quaint or exotic; they think and feel as convincingly as do their white neighbors; their language is man's talk, not the babbling of Brer Rabbit. . . . This is a rare, bountiful book, rich and authentic history and the best of fiction."[21]

A review from a woman's standpoint by Katherine Woods appeared in the *New York Times Book Review*. She wrote:

In this historical novel of the settlement of Australia, the stuff of epic drama is given a living expression that is nobly worthy of its subject. *The Timeless Land* is a novel of towering stature, beautifully molded, soundly and broadly based, penetrating and challenging in its contribution to knowledge. . . . So surely and completely as to leave us almost unaware of her really great achievement she has shown us the white men as the natives saw them, and native life as they themselves felt it to be. . . . Her style is one of depth and resonance rather than vivacity, and its strength and beauty are like organ tones. The lasting value of this novel does not lie, however, in any one facet of story or scene, but in the balance and wholeness of its capacious recreation, which holds every sector firm in its relation to the center, the founding of the new nation in this timeless land.[22]

Milton Rugoff commented in the *New York Herald-Tribune Review of Books:* "Perhaps history deserves the credit for the vertebrae of this narrative, for the outlines of many characters, for the backdrop — the author alone deserves it for the sense of life, of tension and immediacy, for recapturing vividly the spirit of the place, the time and the men who lived through it. . . . Much credit is due the author for resisting the besetting sin of historical fiction — chocolate-icing the unhandsome past with gaudy romance, or the corollary sin, chocolate-sprinkling it with heroes and attractive adventuresomeness. . . . It is, in fact, not Britain alone that is implicitly arraigned here but the entire civilization which blandly assumed that even its worst vices were better than anything alien."[23]

### V  *"An Image of National Identity"*

In London, the *Times Literary Supplement* gave "first choice" among the recommended novels of the week to this important work. "With *The Timeless Land*, Miss Eleanor Dark comes to her full stature," the review begins. "In nothing that she has written until now was there clear evidence of that spaciousness or unity of vision which in the last resort is surely the distinguishing mark of what is called major fiction. . . . Written with strong and deep imagination and with a passion of insight into the historical beginnings of the Australian people, the book has genuine creative force, with here and there a touch of greatness. . . . A nobly conceived and vividly illuminating piece of work."[24]

In her own country, Eleanor Dark was given a highly appreciative first notice in the Sydney *Morning Herald*. "With an unerring selective instinct she has chosen those personalities from the records which best serve to make her picture and her argument vivid and convincing. In order to give the story richness, variety, and that additional detail which adds spice to any historical novel, she has created brilliantly several characters in whom are embodied all those small but vastly important traits which distinguish a man from his fellow, one race from another. One of the most striking features of the novel is its powerful atmospheric suggestiveness. Eleanor Dark writes well. But that is not all. She has, besides, the ability to transport the reader into the very heart of the scenes she describes."[25]

A lengthy essay on the Red Page of the Sydney *Bulletin* attempted to show that the novel suffered because it was overladen with history and politics. "But fiction — the art of the novel — has nothing to do with patriotism. . . . It would be unjust to convey the impression that *The Timeless Land* is only history, only politics." But "The weaknesses of *The Timeless Land* — as fiction; though not as an essay — are due to the dethronement of character in favor of history and political analysis."[26]

Uther Barker, however, early appreciated the eminence of this novel. "Eleanor Dark always writes with distinction, but in *The Timeless Land* she rises to heights hitherto unequalled in ever-recurring passages of exquisite prose. Her affinity for nature, both mystical and functional, has the power to lure her away from her analytical preoccupation into emotion that is spontaneous, direct, and pure where thought and feeling are at last made one, borne irresistibly along upon the rhythm of the unquestioning heart."[27]

Later critics have uniformly praised *The Timeless Land* as an Australian classic. John McKellar wrote in 1948: "She goes to the root of the matter with quite unmelodramatic intensity. *The Timeless Land* is in a genre which has enabled her to throw into higher relief the spiritual dichotomy that really existed and still exists in civilized communities."[28] The same writer concluded in 1954: "Eleanor Dark is the outstanding figure in Australian letters who tries to make history significant within the framework she has chosen to present it."[29]

H. M. Green gives six large pages to Eleanor Dark's *The Timeless Land* and *Storm of Time*, and says of the former:

If the purely invented parts sink farther below the horizon, the re-creation of past life and times, of the characteristics and coloring of the new and almost terrifyingly difficult world as it was then, of the rotton-runged ladder, jagged with barbed wire, up which Phillip and his successors slowly fought their sometimes desperate way, of the character and personality of Phillip; the bold conception and solid base of the book, the breadth and the slow sweep of the creative imagination that constructed it: these combine to make *The Timeless Land* a landmark in Australian historical fiction; and it is not as fiction only that it is important, for it cannot wisely be neglected by students of the first period in Australian history.[30]

Cecil Hadgraft concludes:

These novels are literally historical; indeed, for much of the story the author could, if required, have pointed to documents. For some critics this is a virtue; for others it is an indication that Australian fiction has not grown up. But Eleanor Dark mostly escapes the bias that actuates those novelists trying to prove a case that supports their political beliefs. She is, in addition, a far better writer, a wielder of prose that can at times become almost transparent. And she has a penetration into the motives and passions of men and women that saves her from giving us pasteboard figures. Of the historical writers of this period she is the most considerable.[31]

The following year, Harry Heseltine declared: "In its determination to do honor to black and white, officer and private soldier, freeman and convict, *The Timeless Land* is one of the most comprehensive attempts in Australian fiction to fuse the diverse elements of the past into an image of national identity."[32] Critical comments on Eleanor Dark's trilogy as a whole appear at the end of chapter 8.

Not generally known is the fact that *The Timeless Land* was one of the primary influences in the writing life of the popular novelist James A. Michener, author of *Tales of the South Pacific, Hawaii,* and other books about ethnic conflict. "It was an amazing book, way ahead of its time in its probing back into the aboriginal mind," he wrote to the present author on August 13, 1975, "and it inspired me toward some of the devices I have used with some success. Of all the contemporary novels I would consider [her book] and Joseph Pennell's *History of Rome Hanks* to have been the most formative insofar as my attitudes were concerned, and I would have been very proud to have written either of them. . . . My debt to this woman is enormous."

## CHAPTER 7

# Time of Storm

THE success of *The Timeless Land* was followed, several years later, by the second and third volumes of the trilogy — *Storm of Time* (1948) and *No Barrier* (1954), which carried the story through the eventful year 1814. Mrs. Dark avoided the frequent fate of sequels by continuing the invented actions begun in the first volume and increasing her skill in using documentary sources to advance the narrative on the historical side. Together, the three volumes may be taken as a saga — in the literal sense — of the first quarter of a century of settlement in Australia's first colony, told with historical veracity as well as exciting imaginative adventure. Nor is the thought content neglected, for both the succeeding novels are filled with social commentary.

*Storm of Time* was written between March, 1944, and December, 1947 — a period of almost four years. It is by far the longest book by Mrs. Dark, running to some 350,000 words — the length of three or four average novels. Naturally, there is scope for a number of minor incidents, real and imaginary, and more room for commentary — often ironical — on social adaptation among various conflicting interests in the growing colony.

## I  Shamed by a French Captain

The theme of *Storm of Time* is anticipated at the end of *The Timeless Land*, when Governor Arthur Phillip, departing from the scene of his five years of labor, reflects: "For it had been his task simply to insist upon survival, but now survival was assured, and future governors — himself or others — must face another problem. From now on it would be less the spur of faith that was needed than the curb of wisdom." The problems of the succeeding governors centered around the need for the civil authority to avoid being dominated by the military; for as soon as Phillip sailed for England, Major Francis Grose, head of the New South Wales Corps, took over the rule of the colony and ran it for the benefit of his greedy subordinates.

Logically, the main characters of *Storm of Time* are the three governors that followed Phillip and failed, as he did, to curb the license and acquisitiveness of the soldiery that should have been the main support of the administration. The first is the aging Captain John Hunter, who after five years was willing to yield his office to Philip Gidley King, another of the original band that landed at Sydney Cove in 1788. King was succeeded by Captain William Bligh, survivor of the celebrated mutiny of the *Bounty*. In the fateful year 1808, Bligh was once more to be overthrown, this time by a body of land mutineers under the calculating conspirator John Macarthur.

What is the theme of *Storm of Time*? The "curb of wisdom" was sadly lacking in the colony during the rule of Phillip's three successors. This novel shows at length that the struggle to survive in a new country was almost as severe as the struggle among various factions to gain ascendancy in a new society in the old land. A class system exported from the British Isles suffered a sea change even during the voyages to the antipodes. In an isolated colony of some eight thousand exiles — government officials, soldiers, convicts, ex-convicts, traders, free settlers, and wealthy landholders — the interplay of interests in the first two decades violently created a society different from anything in the Old World. The importance of class — always a fertile theme in British literature — gives way to the importance of a breakdown of conventional social stratification on a frontier. The cultural development of Australia, one may note, differs little in general trends from that of the United States a century or so earlier; and the fierce spirit of independence deriving from generations on a frontier accounts in part for both national attitudes of self-confidence.

In their various ways, the characters realize that the new land has forcefully modified their lives and advanced the breakdown of imported ethics. Governor King sees that the land cries out for different courses: "hope lifted in a new country, ambition enlarged, and hands stretched out to grab. Here was no vast, elaborate structure of government, rooted in centuries of tradition, to quell the murmuring masses . . ." (115).[1] Conor Mannion, the young bride, is shocked that "no barriers" exist in the colony to set apart the lower classes (127). John Macarthur, embodiment of acquisitiveness, sees only "land, land, land — empty land, sun-drenched and grass-covered, its green slopes dotted with thousands upon thousands of woolly, moving shapes — a land virtually untouched and unrealized. A land for plunder . . ." (194). Young Mark Harvey is revolted because he is part of a system in which "meagre rewards of harsh toil and bitter living" are "measured against rich rewards of gentle birth and well-lined pockets" (278). For England has come to Australia. "This is England. Not the land, not the harbor, not the rock pointing at the sky. But the houses, the ships, the gallows on the rock. The greed, the brutality, the strife and the suffering were not born here. They were brought" (279).

The action of *Storm of Time* is extensive, and little can be gained by giving a complete synopsis of the year-by-year events, real and imagined. The main events, however, must be kept in mind if one is to appreciate the unfolding of the themes and the sharpness of characterization and setting.

Book One, "Governor Hunter," opens on January 26, 1799, the eleventh anniversary of the founding of the colony. John Hunter, who had taken over from Grose about two years earlier, is now a man of sixty-two, burdened with a responsibility beyond the powers of a simple sailor. The colony is stagnant, suffering from the diversion of labor to the growing estates of private gentlemen and officers of the New South Wales Corps, who hold a monopoly on trade — especially in liquor, the solace and virtually the currency of the settlement. His chief opponent is Captain John Macarthur, supercilious and arrogant, commanding at the town of Parramatta and proprietor of thriving Elizabeth Farm. In this small colony, any personal encounter becomes an uproar, and gossip and backbiting are the chief forms of amusement. The disturbances are exacerbated by the presence of political prisoners, sent overseas for seditious acts.

Stephen Mannion, who tries to remain neutral, has built a fine new house on the banks of the Nepean River, expecting the arrival of his second wife, Conor Moore, a sixteen-year-old beauty from Ireland. He has employed young Mark Harvey to tutor his sons — Patrick, now fifteen, and Miles, eight. In the household are Ellen Prentice, housekeeper and former mistress, her son Andy and daughter Maria, and black Dilboong, the eight-year-old daughter of Bennilong, chief aboriginal character of *The Timeless Land*. Patrick encounters Ellen's son Johnny, who has been living for years with the native tribes and has inherited his father's outlaw homestead, far across the river from the Mannion estate.

Philip Gidley King with his wife arrives in April, 1800, ready to take over the reins of government, and Hunter sails for England on the *Buffalo*, along with young Patrick Mannion, who will become a London gentleman.

Book II, "Governor King," is the longest of the three sections of the novel, and covers the years from 1800 to 1806. Even Captain George Johnston — no worse an offender than any other officer of the Corps — had been arrested for selling rum to his men, and King is even more eager than Hunter to stamp out the traffic in spirits; but he is slowly worn down by organized resistance and conspiracy. The ringleader, Macarthur, is arrested and sent to England to stand trial for wounding Colonel William Paterson, head of the "Rum Corps," in a duel, but the other officers and most of the tradesmen in the colony continue to enrich themselves by illegal dealing.

Conor has her first child at Christmas time — a girl named Julia. Her husband reverts to his visits to Ellen's cottage, and Johnny, lurking on the estate, filled with hatred for the man who stands in his mind for all oppression, savagely tries to kill him but instead spears Mannion's overseer. Matt Finn, an Irish convict who works on the estate, is flogged for reading Thomas Paine's *Common Sense*, a book filled with revolutionary ideas, but Conor is attracted by him and begins to share his hatred of tyranny. Two French exploring ships visit the settlement, but their reception is marred by King's fear that they might colonize Van Diemen's Land, and he quickly raises the flag there. He is shamed, however, by Captain Nicolas Baudin's remark about the lands belonging to the natives: "You will presently remain the peaceful possessors of their heritage."

## II  *Victor Over Three Governors*

King, the victim of resistance and calumny, cannot depend for support on his lieutenant-governor, Colonel Paterson, who retires from responsibility because of ill health, or Major Johnston, the proud possessor of the estate of Annandale and a follower of Macarthur's cause.

Johnny is wounded during the abortive uprising of the convicts at the government farm at Castle Hill in 1804, and becomes even more an enemy of the exploiters of the downtrodden prisoners. He continues to harass the Mannion estate, and manages to help Finn escape, to join him in his mountain hideout. Finn enlarges the young savage's education and encourages the native clan around the dwelling to increase their property and prepare a refuge for other convicts who might join them.

Macarthur returns from England in June, 1805, as arrogant as ever, "the hero of the fleece," with royal support for his plans to build a wool-exporting industry in New South Wales and with requests for large landholdings in a lush inland district. Harvey, who has become a secretary for Mannion, despises the work he must do, resigns, and opens a small school in Sydney for poor children and the offspring of convicts. Conor talks with him on a visit to the Mannion town house, and continues trying to understand the pattern of the colony. Her scraps of knowledge yield

an ugly, amorphous impression of rapacity and corruption, of hypocrisy, trickery, slander, and intimidation; of a society building up, upon a foundation of felons, a superstructure which sometimes looked uglier than felonry itself, and enforcing its discipline on the lower classes by means which seemed to brand it as lower than they; of a governor whose power, though vested in him by the King, was yet inadequate against the complicated power of wealth; of an insane, contradictory element, its origin obscure and incomprehensible, whereby some who were against the King's representative in New South Wales, nevertheless enjoyed a mysterious support from the King's representatives in England. . . .

Droughts, fires, and floods cause suffering in 1806. Johnny and Finn move further westward to a stronghold in the Wollondilly Valley, following Paine's adjuration to "receive the fugitive, and prepare in time an asylum for mankind." Governor King learns that his successor will be Captain Bligh, and fears that "more than the severity of a tyrant" will be needed to control the growing excesses in Port Jackson.

The action culminates in Book III, "Governor Bligh." This naval officer, accompanied by his daughter Mrs. Mary Putland and her ailing husband, arrives in July. He feels confident that, using "justice, energy, discipline," he can command a colony as well as a ship; but his old failure to prevent a mutiny on the *Bounty* haunts him even in New South Wales. He learns from outgoing Governor King that "no relationship existed between any two classes — and hardly even between any two individuals — which did not contain at least the elements of a feud" (413); and as he energetically surveys his domain he realizes the truth of the statement. He is on a collision course with John Macarthur, and the story clings closely to the recorded accounts of the conflict of personalities leading to the furious events of January, 1808, and the armed deposition of Governor Bligh and his arrest in his own house.[2]

Previous to the collision between Macarthur, the irresistible force, and Bligh, the immovable object, events progress more rapidly on the Nepean. Johnny and Finn explore the heights of the Blue Mountains — presumably the first white men to mount their forbidding summits — and then attack the Mannion estate in an attempt to free the convicts and enlarge their secret force. On the morning when John Macarthur is jailed for defying royal authority, Beltrasna is attacked. Stephen and Patrick — who has returned from Britain to aid his father on the estate — and their servants defeat Johnny and Finn. Finn is captured and hauled off to receive a thousand lashes as punishment. Conor gets him away, but too late — he dies crawling toward freedom. Conor's loveless marriage is at an end when she witnesses the cruelty of Mannion — who gets his just desserts when he is shot to death by Johnny. Ellen takes the blame for her savage son's act, and Patrick becomes the father of a child by Dilboong, daughter of Bennilong. Thus, on the same date, storms of violence take over both the plantation in the country and Government House in the town as the long book ends. Just twenty years have elapsed since the flag of England was first raised over Sydney Cove.

Characterization in *Storm of Time* is, properly, focused on the three governors who represent royal authority in the growing colony. Hunter, the elderly sailor, failed, although he gave all he had — "his genuine goodwill, his sincere humanity, and his plodding, stubborn honesty" were inadequate equipment with which to contend against "the lust for wealth and privilege which had opposed them" (117).

King, a more complex figure, was energetic but "vain and slightly pompous, and he flared easily into irascibililty. He possessed a sharp and sometimes malicious sense of humor, and could turn, on occasion, an ironical phrase which might be witty, but did not stop short of wounding" (113). He was himself vulnerable to lampoons, however, and in the end his achievement was not sufficient to overcome the plots against him. "He had settled large numbers of emancipated convicts on the land, steadily reducing the numbers rationed from the Government store. He had rescued many children from lives of depravity. He had at least embarrassed the monopolists by fixing prices, and encouraging trade from outside the colony to compete with them. He had regulated the currency, brought more public land under cultivation, assisted the settlers to improve their livestock, established new outposts, sponsored new discoveries, promoted small industries. . . . But the military and their adherents were still his powerful foes, and their rancour only increased with prosperity . . ." (400).

William Bligh is the most sympathetic character in the book — perhaps a surprising statement for those who have seen him only as a monster of tyranny in film versions of the famed *Bounty* mutiny. Now, in his early fifties, he is a commanding figure who knows both his faults and his strengths.

He acknowledged his impatience, his irritability, the arrogance of his pride, the violence of his temper, the mischief often wrought by his eloquent and ungovernable tongue. Yet he knew that these were the faults of his virtues. Filled with a passion for efficiency, he was impatient of slovenly performance; driving himself without mercy, his irritation flared against idleness; knowing his own qualities, he felt contempt for those who did not share them; conscious always of the responsibilities of his command, his rage loosed itself against those who failed him, and his tongue flayed them with bitter words. He admitted his explosive temper as a fault, but held with stubborn pride that it did not explode unprovoked; and there remained always at the root of his self-analysis a wondering sense of outrage that it should be provoked so often. For he was a good commander. He knew that, not only from searching his heart, but as a fact supported by the most ruthless examination of his behavior. (423)

Bligh's lacking sense of humor opened himself and his family to suffering from real or imagined slights. He was no coward; and Mrs. Dark gives perhaps the best interpretation of his behavior when, hiding from his enemies in the hope of escaping to the Hawkesbury settlements, he took refuge under a bed in an upper room of Government House. His strategy after his deposition — refusing to be shipped off from the scene while his gloating foes plunder the region and take revenge on his supporters — is justified by the ponderings that conclude the novel. "The final judge was truth — immortal" (590). Some day it would bring his adversaries to justice.

John Macarthur is, however, an even bolder figure, whose effrontery and cunning make him more than a match even for Bligh. Still in his early thirties, he has risen from a penniless lieutenant to become a landed proprietor with a growing family and a finger in every pie in the colony. His almost insane egotism brings him to great heights and eventually will lapse into madness. "Active opposition was an outrage never to be forgiven or forgotten. His temper was violent, but cold; his enmities bitter, cherished — strong currents running steadily beneath the ice of an outward self-control" (32). At the root of his antagonism to the government that he was pledged to serve is his ambition as a trader and farmer. It is "a spiritual necessity not only to be always in the right, but to be acknowledged so; not only to be guiltless, but to be injured and persecuted; not only to be thus wronged, but to appear loftily magnanimous under injury and persecution" (179). King had warned the incoming governor, Bligh, against Macarthur: "With the manner of a turtle-dove, the cunning of a fox, the stubbornness of a mule, and the rapacity of a shark!" (433). And as King wrote to his superior in London, when sending Macarthur home under arrest: "I need not inform you who or what Captain Macarthur is. He came here in 1790 more than £ 500 in debt, and is now worth at least £ 20,000 . . . there are no resources which art, cunning, and a pair of basilisk eyes can afford that he does not put into practice to obtain any point he undertakes. . . . I shall close the subject by observing that if Captain Macarthur returns here in any official character, it should be that of Governor, as one-half the colony belongs to him, and it will not be long before he gets the other half" (181). But King's dispatches are destroyed before they reach London, and Macarthur returns to the colony in triumph — victor over Hunter, King, and, in the upshot, Bligh.

Stephen Mannion in middle age is still a hateful person who cannot win young Conor's love and treats his laborers like cattle. His son Patrick benefits little from his life in London and is more interested in writing poems than in managing a farm. The younger son, Miles, soon leaves the settlement for London.

## III   A Novel That Pays Dividends

Conor and Mark Harvey, who first appear in Storm of Time, gradually fall in love. A chit of sixteen with gray-blue eyes, smooth black hair, and a rosy complexion, she develops at her crisis, leaning over the dying Finn, into a social critic, "vaguely seeking some ratification by her brain of the emotion so frighteningly aroused in her — condemnation and abhorrence of the whole machinery of her society. She searched — and found nothing . . ." She who had cherished the scraps of writing by Tom Paine has become a rebel, seeking the freedom offered by the new land. Harvey's rough reeducation has preceded hers, and together they will try to repair some of the havoc wrought by the system.

Johnny, the convict boy who becomes a native, also develops in this book. Taught to write by Tom Towns, the consumptive outlaw, and later indoctrinated by Matt Finn, he discovers the world of learning, and his sympathies swing from tribal allegiance to aggressive acts against the oppressors. However, he keeps in touch with the aborigines and his half brother Billalong, uses them in his plans, and marries a young widow, Ngili, by whom he has a half-caste son.

The natives, however, play only a modest role in this sequel. Dilboong also mothers a half-caste. Pemulwy is drawn from a real person — the last fighter against white intrusion, who has the honor of having his pickled head sent to London. With him, steady resistance by local tribesmen ceases in the Port Jackson area.

Ellen Prentice's sacrifice of her life to draw suspicion away from Johnny is a melodramatic deed. Eleanor Dark uses the other women characters, however, to reveal her conviction that the female side of pioneer life should not be overlooked. Portraits are given of Mrs. King, Mary Putland (who tried to defend her father, Governor Bligh, with a parasol against a corps of soldiery), and especially Elizabeth Macarthur (who reared a large family and successfully operated the family estate during the years of her husband's absence). Such personalities did not need the protection that was supposed to be offered them by courtly gentlemen, trying to shelter them from sordid knowledge. Mrs. King had survived mutiny at Norfolk Island and half a dozen perilous times on the ocean and had borne three children at the island and another at sea.

A dozen other colonial figures appear in the book at more or less length: reluctant Colonel Paterson; easygoing George Johnston; the Reverend Richard Johnson and his colleague Samuel Marsden, the flogging parson of Parramatta; the drunken judge-advocate Richard Atkins; the Irish seditionists; Howe, editor of the *Sydney Gazette*; and young William C. Wentworth, who will appear at greater length in *No Barrier*. Even a visiting Maori chief from New Zealand, Tip-a-he, is mentioned. At times, indeed, the story resounds with what might be considered the small gossip of a colonial outpost.

The setting of *Storm of Time* is again the Port Jackson region, but its borders stretch farther inland, even to the mountains that beckoned in *The Timeless Land*. The growing community becomes familiar to the reader. The town, in the eyes of Bligh, who had come to spend some years governing it, has "an air of awkward immaturity, at once pathetic and repellent" (426). The quest of Johnny and Finn for freedom on the rooftops of the mountain chain gives Eleanor Dark a chance to describe the blueness of the valleys where "even the ordinary processes of seeing took on a new quality" (451).

The style of *Storm of Time* is a notable change from that of its predecessor in the series. Perhaps as a reaction from unfavorable comments by reviewers on her use of the introspective method, the author utilizes most of the time herein a form of straight narrative, and the book now and then even reverts to chronicle.

Reviews of *Storm of Time* may have enjoyed a "halo effect" resulting from the success of *The Timeless Land*, but most comments accepted the big sequel on its own terms. The Australian edition appeared earlier than the American one. The reviewer in the Sydney *Morning Herald* said of the author, in part: "She gets right inside the times to let us walk wholeheartedly along the bullock tracks beside the Tank Stream, peering now into dingy scattered shops of the town or cabins of the country, and now into Government House, where governors fidget while John Macarthur plots. . . . Governor Bligh comes out of the novel a human and understandable character. . . . But then most of the other characters of history that come to life here become understandable, too. That makes it such a notable piece of historical fiction."[3]

A lengthy notice on the Red Page of the Sydney *Bulletin* found Mannion and Johnny to be unconvincing and stated that the novel was a dramatization of ideas or an "historical essay in fictional form," but gave credit for several characterizations.

Governors Hunter and King, unremarkable men, are remarkably well presented, and Bligh, the liveliest figure in the book, is completely convincing. . . . One of the book's best scenes is when Bligh, confronted with a lampoon, suddenly stares at nothing, seeing in his mind the face of Fletcher Christian. . . . Conor, Mannion's second wife . . . is chiefly a mouthpiece for the author's criticisms of the brutalities of the period; yet, through her, shadowy as she is, Eleanor Dark brings the novel to its deepest humanity and its most moving episode: when, in Conor's attempts at sympathetic gestures to the convict Finn there is shown the terrible, unpassable chasm between the fettered convict and the representative, however unwilling she may be, of the tyranny that has chained him.[4]

An article on the historical aspects of the novel stated: "It will take rank among the foremost novels produced by writers of this country. It could, however, have been a great novel judged by the standards of any country at any time. . . . When Eleanor Dark writes of the land, Australia, and its native inhabitants, she achieves greatness."[5] A lengthy critique by Uther Barker in *Southerly* terms the book "a work not only impressive but authentic, a book not merely of fact and fiction, but also for reference and rediscovery. On this plane *Storm of Time* equally with *The Timeless Land*, its predecessor, is a valuable contribution to the corpus of Australian literature at its highest level."[6]

American reviewers were equally laudatory. "If any belated doubt lingered that Australian literature has come of age," opened a notice in the *Herald-Tribune*, "this novel would dispel it. It is a long but never tedious, solidly detailed but nervously moving, honestly violent but not melodramatic, story of the tortured beginnings of the British penal colony at Botany Bay."[7] The *New York Times Book Review* concluded: "As history and anthropology this book is impressive and convincing — as fiction it is exhausting. For romance, that staple ingredient of good recent historical fiction, Mrs. Dark finds little space in some six hundred pages. Yet *Storm of Time* is carefully and painstakingly written, dramatic and moving in many of its episodes."[8] The *Christian Science Monitor* notice concluded: "*Storm of Time* is a novel which fulfills its purpose in leaving with the reader a realization of the clashing interests, mistakes, progress, and retardments of those early years, and more than all else, of the individuality of Australia as a land, founded by Englishmen but not English, molded by its topography and its vast resources, able to outride the storms."[9] The *Saturday Review of Literature* remarked: "It is an historical novel (in the richest meaning of that term) which is alive with people and events. And if it is sometimes turgid it is never lacking in strength. It is a very long time since I have read a novel that kept me up so late or claimed my attention so completely. . . . What is to the point is that here is a solid, leisurely novel that pays handsome dividends in pleasure and knowledge."[10]

## CHAPTER 8

# Time of Striving

THE last volume of the Dark trilogy, *No Barrier*, appeared in 1953 — a dozen years after the first volume. It covers the first few years of the viceregal sway of Governor Lachlan Macquarie, who had been sent to bring order and progress to the chaotic colony.

In many ways, *No Barrier* is properly a sequel to *Storm of Time* and, in comparable style, continues that story for another four hundred pages. The theme is close to that of the earlier volume, except that *No Barrier* shows how a military officer, as governor, could wield the civil power and even recommend the transfer of his own regiment to India after a few years and its replacement by another regiment without local attachments. However, the class struggle continues — this time most crucially during the governor's attempt to give the "emancipist" group (those convicts who had served their terms and had achieved success) a social equality with the "exclusives" (the free settlers who had snobbishly set up an elite system). But, as will be discussed further, the high point of *No Barrier*, as its title implies, is the opening of a gateway through the confining mountain range, marking the end of the first phase of settlement and the beginning of a continent-wide epic of land conquest. A tight class structure could not endure when any man might pack his possessions on his back and trudge across the Blue Mountains into a lush interior where he could claim as his own a grazing domain as far as eye could see.

I   *A Route Still Followed Today*

The future of the Australian people is predicted by Conor Mannion, who is closest to an author's mouthpiece in this novel, when she responds to Laetitia's doubts about the improvement of the convict class. "I should expect to see no sudden transformation," Conor asserts. "Yet if all these remedies should be applied patiently and for as long as were needful, I think it might be found that a miracle had occurred — not only affecting the children or grandchildren of those whom you despise, but our own also" (275).[1] The remedy was fated to be slow, for New South Wales remained a penal colony until 1840.

The action of *No Barrier* picks up where *Storm of Time* leaves off, in February, 1808, just after the deposition of Governor Bligh. For those readers unfamiliar with the previous book, the device is used of having a synopsis given through quotations from the journal of Conor Mannion. Political as well as domestic events are related through the end of 1809, when the new governor, Colonel Lachlan Macquarie, arrives with his wife and staff to put the disordered colony into shape.

Macquarie begins early in 1810 his task of replacing the New South Wales Corps with his own regiment. He is the perfect administrator that the colony had previously lacked, and his wife is the perfect helpmate, despite her inability to bear live children. He plans to make the village into a proper town, with wide streets and imposing buildings. He controls the growing colonial trade, and even harnesses the liquor traffic by giving a three-year monopoly to several gentlemen who promise to build a hospital on the hill above the harbor — the "Rum Hospital" which brought him a reprimand from London but which is still standing today on Macquarie Street in Sydney.

The Macquaries visit Patrick Mannion, now the master of the Beltrasna estate, who still feels guilt concerning his playmate Johnny Prentice, even though Patrick is sure Johnny murdered Stephen Mannion. Johnny has continued living in his mountain retreat with his native wife and child, but fears that the advance of exploration will reveal his hideout, and his old hatred of the white oppressors begins once more to smoulder.

Conor, living with her two children in the Sydney town house, is approaching the age of thirty. She overcomes the humble objections of Mark Harvey, marries him, moves into the cottage where his school is thriving, and studies household arts. As she says, idleness can be a burden to an active person, and in Sydney there are opportunities even for a woman of her class to live usefully. The pair are married at St. Phillip's Church (where Eleanor Dark's grandfather was later to be canon) and employ an orphan girl, Emily, to help Conor in the house. Conor's daughter Julia dislikes Harvey and sails off, to be pampered by relatives in Ireland. As the year ends, a son is

born to the Harveys, but Johnny's son dies in the bush and his wife
leaves the place, as is the native custom after a death.

Early in 1812, Gregory Blaxland visits Patrick Mannion and speaks
of the need for more cattle-grazing land, which he hopes to find
beyond the barrier of the Blue Mountains. The conquest of this
obstacle, which has not been penetrated although Sydney had been
founded almost a quarter of a century earlier, had also attracted the
interest of William C. Wentworth and Lieutenant Lawson.

Suffering guilt, Patrick decides to find Johnny, who meanwhile
has crossed the Blue Mountains and fears that the only route through
them lies in his secret valley. The pair meet, and Johnny shoots
Patrick in the leg, but is spared when Patrick gains the upper hand
and throws both muskets over a cliff. When Johnny hears that his
native wife has been attacked and killed by three white settlers, he
vows to avenge her. One of the three has just become the bigamous
husband of Emily, Conor's maid. This sadistic bully, Joseph Dean, is
taking Emily in his cart to his farm when Johnny murders him and
carries off Emily, the only witness. Overcoming their differences,
this pair live together in the mountain hut, and Johnny is partly
domesticated in spite of himself.

Miles Mannion — now a six-foot-five gentleman of great energy
and a boisterous laugh — returns. from England with his bride, the
former Laetitia ffoulkes, and speaks of his old determination to conquer the mountain barrier. Governor Macquarie, returning fatigued
from a visit to the subsidiary colony at Van Diemen's Land, is
troubled by the parsimony of the Colonial Office in London. He is
still determined to build a fine town and to extend roads in many
directions from Sydney Cove, but he is also hampered by the
vestiges of old strife and by the refusal of the contemptuous free
settlers to accept equality with the emancipists. "A quarrel between
a soldier and a sailor speedily became a quarrel between the Army
and the Navy; a disagreement between a settler and a convict was
soon an issue between the free population and the felonry; a dispute
involving a native was apt to take on the aspect of inter-racial war;
and should His Excellency find himself (as he often did) at variance
with Mr. Marsden, there was even, in the reverend gentleman's attitude, a suggestion that the temporal power was presuming to array
itself against the hosts of Heaven" (232). Tillers of the land had
developed, despite adversities, a surplus of produce in a place where
famine had once reigned; but now arose the problem of finding a
suitable market that would not rival the chartered East India Com-

pany and the merchants of Mother England. And, ironically, one possibility was distilling liquor from the surplus grain.

In 1813, the year of Bennilong's death, Laetitia, who fears the "miserable, dirty, naked savages," asks that Dilboong be sent away from Beltrasna. The aboriginal daughter of Bennilong kills herself rather than suffer separation from her idol, Miles. Miles is determined to be "first" to cross the mountain barrier, and manages to meet with Johnny, who is persuaded to be his guide. Paradoxically, if he uses Johnny's hut as a base and follows Johnny's river route, he cannot claim the glory of discovery, because he has promised not to reveal the location of the hideaway. The range had previously been crossed by Johnny and Finn, and in any event, as Johnny says, "There's been natives crossin' back and forth for maybe hundreds of years." Despite hazards, Miles does penetrate the range and decides to erect a baronial mountain home on a plateau above Johnny's farm, "flamboyantly poised between the coastal settlements and the rich inland," on a site that would lie beside the road eventually to be built.

The historic expedition led by Geoffrey Blaxland, W. C. Wentworth, and Lieutenant Lawson is briefly described in dramatic style.[2] Macquarie does not wish to have his limited domain suddenly transformed into the threshold of a continent open to settlement, but he has Assistant Surveyor Evans lay out a road route into the interior, following closely on the precipitous Blaxland trail that today is also the route of a railway.

II  *"Something White, Soft, and Soundless"*

Evans and his party greet the eventful year 1814 from the crest of the Blue Mountains. In July, William Cox, a former paymaster of the New South Wales Corps, is appointed to build a road across the mountains to the fertile grazing plains beyond. The work of a dozen artisans and a gang of convict laborers led by the dynamic Cox, the road pushes along the spine of the mountains and across many ravines and streams in a few winter months, in spite of obstacles that make the story a triumph of frontier achievement. At the end of the year, Cox, who has supervised the building of "some hundred miles of good serviceable road," sits on the banks of the Fish River amid lush plains and writes: "December 29. A fine morning, which the birds seem most to enjoy on the banks of the river. The shrubs and flowers are also extremely fragrant. Left six men preparing materials for the bridge across the main river . . ." (384).

Several critics have felt that *No Barrier* does not end the series with a great climax, but that the story merely stops. Yet there are few loose ends, or futures that cannot be guessed. Questions remain that might be answered in a possible fourth volume. But it seems likely that the crossing of the Blue Mountains would be, to Mrs. Dark — who had lived almost all her life in the heart of these rugged hills — a fitting climax to the saga of the first quarter-century of settlement. In *The Timeless Land,* published a dozen years earlier than *No Barrier,* Governor Phillip is shown to be aware of the challenge of the interior, and in the first year of his rule he leads an exploring party whose members look at each other and realize that "this was the end of the coastal and the beginning of the inland stage" (102). In 1814, Governor Macquarie realizes that "the pushing forward of this new land frontier was by far the most important and exciting of all the things he had seen happen here. It was an end — and a beginning. The colony could never be the same again" (338 - 39). The timeless land had appropriated the conquerors, and a new frontier was open for at least a century. The Australians, as they were beginning to call themselves, "would have to forget that the sea had once been always at their backs, an escape route, a line of retreat, a reminder to nostalgic hearts that home was far away. . . . They had made a little gaol for felons, but now they were all prisoners, and their sentence was to learn that their gaol could be a heritage" (339). A generation has passed, and the new start is also symbolized by the births of many children — among them not only Conor Mannion's issue and the brood of pioneer Emily, nor Patrick's half-black daughter of Dilboong, but the native-born son, after many disappointments, of Lachlan Macquarie. The future belongs to this new generation, the "cornstalks," the "currency lads."

Colonel Lachlan Macquarie is, rightly, the dominant figure in *No Barrier.* He is a pious patriarch, a "good ruler," and hence easily resolves most of the challenges that face him, thus lessening the impact of possible dramatic conflicts. *No Barrier* covers, however, only the first five years of his administration, when his fine achievements were most visible and before the troubles arose that were to lead to his replacement in 1821. In the novel, the future challenges are only suggested, as for instance in the attitudes of the legal-minded Bent brothers and in the temptations to spend offered by the availability of the gifted architect-convict Francis Greenway. "There must be new roads, new stores, new barracks, new churches, whole new towns. . . . He would build and build" (75).

Arriving on the eve of the year 1810, Governor Macquarie, a tall and broad-shouldered Scotsman, is impressive in his scarlet and gold braid. "Many years of service in India had darkened his complexion; his unpowdered brown hair was plentiful, brushed up upon his head, adding to his appearance of height; and beneath thick eyebrows his dark eyes were keen and quick" (33). He seems effortlessly to do the wise thing, and is disturbed only by domestic crises like the failure to have his wife give birth to an heir of the clan. Like Bligh a servant to "duty," Macquarie was "no believer in equality, and the years had not mitigated the abhorrence with which, long ago, he had once written of 'the infernal and destructive principles of Democracy' " (262). Yet he knew by 1813 that "a strong and vindictive opposition to himself was gaining strength among the higher ranks. . . . His mind, neither complex nor adventurous, could conceive no alternative to a society breeding crime from harshness, suppressing it with harsh punishment and thus breeding more crime — but it was, within the limitations imposed by such an acceptance, an intelligent mind, and a just one. Intelligence showed him the impossibility of keeping the emancipist class in perpetual segregation, and his sense of justice recoiled from the very thought of attempting it" (263). His rulership of New South Wales was a period of consolidation and steady progress, and he is justly remembered as "the Father of Australia."

The other characters in the book continue to be themselves. Conor Harvey, as the wife of a schoolmaster, has the busy life she so ardently desired. She becomes a prototype of Caroline Chisholm, an admired pioneer woman of history. In her little parlor Conor listens to "tales of poverty, illness, desertion, cruelty, drunkenness, and prostitution" and offers sympathy when the purse of charity cannot "balance the deprivations of the dispossessed." Yet she is impatient with the slowness of social reform, even though the stirred mind provides an "accumulating reservoir of facts and knowledge upon which other minds, goaded by uneasy hearts, could draw" (314).

The most goaded mind is that of Patrick, whose sense of guilt leads to much suffering by others and who, on the eve of departure for Ireland because of his love for his brother's wife, is disposed of by a convict footpad. Miles, his brother, is a more attractive figure — tall, energetic, and optimistic, the prototype of the inland explorer. The brothers run the finest estate in the colony next to that of the absent John Macarthur and have the entrée into the highest society, so that they form a link between the settlers and the townspeople.

Many a name among the revered pioneers of Australia appears in the pages of *No Barrier*, although few are characters developed to any degree.

Mrs. Dark's interest in female pioneers led her to introduce a new character in this volume — Emily, the orphan-asylum girl who becomes Conor's maid and, by a melodramatic turn of events, the white mate for Johnny, outlaw of the wilds, who as the book ends plans, along with his half-white brother Billalong, to become the bush-ranging scourge of travelers on the new highway. Laetitia, the pale blond wife of Miles, is a weak figure to match the weak nature of the brother she should have married. The wives of Sydney officials — Mrs. Macquarie and the rest — form a sort of colonial chorus in the story.

Mrs. Dark's descriptive powers are given further expression in *No Barrier*, and again the town is contrasted with the bush. Governor Macquarie's delight in transforming the squalid village of Sydney into an impressive landscape is evident throughout, and he is at his best when laying the foundation stone of the new hospital or plotting new streets to be named for Bent, O'Connell, the royal dukes, and himself and his wife. Especially good are the evocations of the city and the market through the eyes of Emily (see pages 98 - 99 and 143).

The majesty and terror of the Blue Mountains, Eleanor Dark's chosen homeplace, are even more impressively depicted.

That night it was bitterly cold, and Gheeger-Gheeger was abroad. He roared and raged through the treetops that overhung the rock shelter where Billalong and Dyonn-ee crouched by a small fire; towards morning he retreated, leaving a strange, unnatural hush behind him, and at dawn Billalong, with a sharp exclamation of wonder and fear, saw plain evidence of sorcery in the sky. It was not rain that was falling, but something white, soft, and soundless which had covered the ground while they lay shivering in an uneasy half-sleep; the naked flesh, touching it, recoiled from a coldness which seemed to burn. He was reassured — though not reconciled — when Dyonn-ee told him that he had seen such a thing before when he had come with Finn to these heights; he gave it a name, and declared that in the lands from which the Beerewolgal came it was frequently seen. (160)

III   *The Trilogy Becomes a Monument*

Expectations of reviewers may have been high in 1953, when *No Barrier* finally was published — in Sydney only, for there was never an American edition. Disappointment followed when it was found that the novel was an extension of *Storm of Time* into the early years of Governor Macquarie. To be sure, the lengthy review in the Melbourne *Age* began by stating that "Eleanor Dark has done more to make ordinary readers acquainted with Australian history than has any Australian historian." But the notice continued with an essay on the fact that convicts and aborgines were the most important element in early society and these had not been given proper weight in the novel; nor had Macquarie been a humanitarian reformer in every way. Concerning the plot, the reviewer felt that soap opera had been rivalled and that a fourth volume would resolve such dangling questions as "Will Conor . . . regain the Mannion millions? Can Miles keep Laetitia in the colony? How can Emily rear her brood in that Crusoe set-up? What will Governor Macquarie do about Judge-Advocate Bent?"[3]

The *Bulletin* reviewer was generally unimpressed, but Sidney Baker in the *Morning Herald* examined at length the possibility that the trilogy was the "Great Australian Novel" — at least, until a better claimant was established. "There will be no dispute" runs the review "that these three books (a collective total of some 700,000 words) are installments of a single story pursued on the twin levels of fact and fiction. . . . Indeed, for anyone wishing to find some easy approach to Australia's early history, these three books are quite unrivalled for their close-packed information."[4] The review in the Adelaide *News* assumed that a fourth volume would appear: "The author works on a large canvas. The concept of the whole, of which this novel is only a part, is even larger. If she tends towards the melodramatic in some of her situations, this was the spirit of the times. Here is an impressive and scholarly novel. The completed series will be a notable contribution to Australian literature."[5]

A lengthy review on the Red Page of the *Bulletin* observed: "When it has these patches of life, and when as a whole the novel has the three-fold appeal of moving easily through another section of Australian history, of painting graceful and sympathetic portraits of women, whether fictional such as Mrs. Mannion and Emily or historical such as Mrs. Macquarie and Mrs. Macarthur, and of telling a romantic adventure-story in the vein of *Robinson Crusoe* through the career of Johnny Prentice, there is no reason why *No Barrier* should not be as popular as its predecessors in Mrs. Dark's series — both of which were Australian best-sellers."[6] A laudatory notice by a historian in *Meanjin Quarterly* stated: "We find once again that Mrs. Dark has immersed herself in her period so extraordinarily well, and has conveyed her feelings so vitally, that as one reads one almost expects to find oneself in the dilapidated streets of Sydney in the early days of Governor Macquarie," and commended in particular the treatment of the native people and the convict class.[7] A long review in another Sydney newspaper said in part: "Its faults, however, are swamped by the power of the novel as a whole, as it goes about its proper task of illuminating the life of its period. And it keeps a nice balance between the history-book material and the possible lives of people not important enough for the historian but vital to the growth of the nation — and pretty much like any of us might be in their circumstances."[8] The reviewer in the *Daily Mail* had the impression that "the author of *No Barrier* has found it harder to keep Macquarie and the personages of his government in proper proportion, as was the case when she dealt with the times of Hunter, King, and Bligh. Except in this one direction, Mrs. Dark has written an entertaining and informative story. Her gift for characterization, her descriptive writing, and her flair for incident are as strong as ever."[9]

Comments on the trilogy as a whole became more appreciative as time passed. Sidney Baker wrote of Mrs. Dark, in "The Great Australian Novel?":

She is, for example, not always easy to read. She offers some outstanding descriptive passages, but there are long gaps between them. She has a keen and sensitive understanding of many of the people about whom she writes — the natives, especially — but we are kept moving too fast through crowded scenes to draw close to all of them. We have a feeling, too, that she tends to play down the discontents of the convicts and to look at our history through the eyes of officials to whom the sufferings of convicts were irrelevant. . . . On the other hand, when we look over the uneven field of our fiction, there is almost nothing that can be compared with this series for its scope, accuracy, and sincerity.[10]

A few days later the Red Page reviewer conceded: "Certainly, with the writing always distinguished, the intellectual standard, if tinged with Leftism, high, and with so many years of our history now covered with steadfast purpose, the sequence deserves the respect of a major undertaking in Australian fiction. . . . Of course it could be argued that in the sequence as a whole Mrs. Dark is really more concerned with the history of New South Wales than with the story of the Mannions; or that in the broadest and longest view the family saga and the history of the colony are inevitably linked; but they would need to be linked more closely, more intimately, more organically, to make this novel satisfying as a work of art."[11] A later notice in the *Bulletin* averred that "It is a rewarding effort to read and re-assess them [the novels of the trilogy] as a unity, for, with all its faults, this composite work has no Australian rival in its scope, depth of research, and sporadic brilliance. Nor, I think, has any other novelist shown quite so clearly the implications of white settlement for the aborigines or interpreted as skillfully our early history through aboriginal eyes. For this kind of roundness, we have only these books to set beside the vast mass of good-quality American frontier writing."[12]

A detailed discussion of the historical content of the trilogy opened with the remarks that there is a "vital distinction between the scores of novels written with some phase of history as their subject-matter and the historical novel which seeks to *interpret* history to us, not merely to write a story. . . . Eleanor Dark is the outstanding figure in Australian letters who tries to make history significant within the framework she has chosen to present it."[13]

In his history of Australian literature, Cecil Hadgraft concludes, concerning the trilogy: "Despite a suspicion of the chronicle, these novels are the most substantial and successful of their kind that we have."[4] The monumental history by H. M. Green (1961) devotes no less than six large pages to the first two volumes (he was unable to include *No Barrier* in his survey). On the occasion of the reprinting in 1963 of the three volumes of the Dark trilogy in a standard format, a reassessment by a sound critic stated that the edition presents

some 1,400 closely-printed pages of the most substantial contribution to the art of historical fiction that this country has seen — even, if the day of the three-decker has passed, perhaps the most substantial contribution it will ever see. . . .

Re-reading the trilogy comes as a shock. One has forgotten how skillfully written, how enjoyable, how interesting, and how moving these books are. The reason for this forgetfulness lies in the theme itself. No historical novelists anywhere before Eleanor Dark had a story so significant to the people they were writing for — the establishment *ab initio* of a society which overran a continent in a century, and the best-documented colonization in history at that. . . . Eleanor Dark took the first quarter-century of Australian history, and determined to get it *all* down on paper. There is an element of piety about the work which affected the way it was received: it has become almost an ancient monument of its own.[15]

A recent reappraisal by a senior tutor in Australian history at the Australian National University admits that it is not correct to say that Eleanor Dark's body of work has been completely neglected. "There is always *The Timeless Land* (1941), which is the first part of a trilogy dealing in semi-factual form with the first years of European settlement in Australia. Indeed, the Australian Broadcasting Commission holds the television rights to this trilogy and has plans to make fifteen one-hour episodes for its first color TV series some time around 1975. The trilogy is all that remains in print and *The Timeless Land* still appears on reading lists for senior school students."[16]

Yes, it is likely that reassessment of the contribution of Eleanor Dark to the literature of her country will guarantee her a high place in critical esteem; and much of her qualification will derive from the creation of the "timeless trilogy," which put on paper the achievements, real and imagined, of the first quarter-century of the settlement of New South Wales.

## CHAPTER 9

# Times of Shadow and Sunshine

**P**UBLICATION of the historical trilogy was interrupted, once, by the appearance of a contemporary Dark novel, *The Little Company* (1945). The title, a quotation from "The Song of Roland" concerning the defenders of Christendom against the Saracens, presumably refers to the seven million Australians who lived through the early years of World War II. A much smaller company, however, is presented in the persons of the Massey family of Sydney and their friends during this troubled time. As Aunt Bee expresses it to herself: "Against the terrific backcloth of human chaos and endeavor which their interminable discussions conjured up, she saw not only Phyllis, but herself and all the rest of them shrink till they became not negligible but undoubtedly very small" (309).[1]

No less than five of these people are writers of books. Writing a novel about a writer is usually considered a desperate tactic, for most readers do not find the agonies or outpourings of a writer of romantic interest or even of concern. Still less exciting as a main character is a writer writing about being unable to write. "It is a stock theme. . . . And, in the second place, the theme can hardly be of more than clinical interest. It is the history of a disease . . . and is likely to become as tedious as any other long-drawn-out account of an illness."[2]

## I *Drama or Chronicle?*

"Creative paralysis" or "writer's block" is undoubtedly common, and undoubtedly Mrs. Dark, like many others, felt an overwhelming frustration during the second global conflict in a lifetime. Seven years intervened between the publication of *The Timeless Land* and its sequel, *Storm of Time*; and in this period Mrs. Dark issued only *The Little Company*. The period during which Gilbert Massey, its leading character, is unable to write his eighth novel extends also for seven years; significantly, the wellsprings of "inspiration" break forth again when he discovers that, unknown to him during the scribblings of his dry years, he had written half a book about his protagonist-to-be. Perhaps all that is needed to cure a case of writer's block is to discover that, after all, one has the material for another book. What is requisite is a subject — if not the early settlement of New South Wales, at least the life of an unrecognized liberal thinker.

The main interest of *The Little Company* lies in its relation to the development of its author, and in its contribution to her comments on the art and craft of authorship. A number of opinions are expressed throughout — particularly on her usual concerns with education, politics, unemployment, class antagonism, pacifism, feminism, and liberalism — but the main theme seems to be the world's neglect of its artists, primarily literary artists, who serve as a sort of warning system to unappreciative humanity.

Gilbert Massey, aged forty-five in 1941, wonders why anyone should bother to write about the disgusting human race. "It's as if the plot had been worked out at the beginning of time. . . . Human History, a comedy-drama in five hundred million acts! Characters in the order of their appearance — the Inert Onlooker, the Reactionary, the Revolutionary Idealist. . . . He saw the Inert Onlooker being hauled and pushed and bustled this way and that by the other two principal characters, but he told himself sourly that there never had been, nor would there be now, any climax, any denouement. He knew that the curtain would fall upon the Onlooker, still gaping in glassy-eyed equanimity, while the others, behind his back and far, far beyond his consciousness, would remain locked in an endless, unresolved struggle" (289). Those who are not onlookers must either take extreme sides or get out of the scene. "Conform or get out. And searching for progress in those past centuries, one found it always in points of departure; in the minds and actions of the people who — got out" (310). The artist, always a nonconformist even though Marxism might take over the world, could wring from the boring, existential contemplation of life one ironic satisfaction — the recording of unpleasant reality. "There was logic behind every event, and direction in every development," Massey concludes at the end, "so that it became a spectacle which one watched, but in which, too, one's own comprehension was a factor. There was, indeed, nothing left of life but this straining, unceasing effort toward comprehension" (318). As Cecil Hadgraft was to write: "The theme of the story is that we must be prepared to face reality: no relationship is purely personal. Any character who does not recognize this truth is either stupid, or neurotic, or egoistic, and is punished by the author accordingly."[3]

The philosophy behind this book, then, is twentieth-century naturalism: the attitude expresses pessimistic determinism, insistence on the meanness of human life, the failure of the individual to influence his society, the pressures of base instinct, the impossibility of progress, the shackles of heredity. The plight of the people therein is not tragic, but merely unfortunate. Still, the writer can achieve a wry triumph by expressing his feelings about the failure of humanity — that is, if he can overcome his inertia and write. In *The Little Company*, almost all the characters are failures, victims of social paralysis, and hence the reader can expect little action, even of an indecisive kind.

The action in the book is barely worthy of the name of plot. The period embraced in Book I extends from the Australian autumn of 1941 to December 7, date of the Japanese attack on Pearl Harbor; Book II encompasses the entire critical year of 1942 — the year when the balance of world power swung mightily from utter catastrophe to the first glimmers of victory for the free nations. The scope dwindles to the affairs of the Massey family at this time, who in their situation on the fringe of the conflict are made to seem like insects on an anthill. What can their actions do to influence anything?

As in earlier books, flashbacks are used to reveal past events that condition present behavior by the cast. One learns that William Massey, who founded a religious-book business in Sydney, married a missionary and built a home called Glenwood on the well-to-do slopes of the North Shore, across the harbor from the city of Sydney. The couple had three children: Gilbert, Martha or Marty, and, belatedly, Nick, whose mother died in childbirth. In a neighboring suburban cottage lived the family of Scott Laughlin, whose daughter Janet played with the two older Massey children. Laughlin encouraged all three to exercise their writing talents. He was an unsuccessful Laborite candidate for public office, was deserted by his wife, and died early, followed to the grave by Janet. His wife married Jerrold Kay, a successful cartoonist,[4] and after his death lived on with their daughter, Elsa Kay, in daily recollection of her life with Laughlin.

Gilbert and Nick manage the inherited book business and along with Marty take some part in the literary life of the metropolis. Marty, who has married Richard Ransom — an elderly, middle-class

Englishman with a genial, too-open mind — is a cynical feminist. Nick is a committed Marxist, who spouts the party line as if he were a phonograph record, but who serves his country in the jungles of New Guinea. Gilbert has published seven novels; but his most recent one, now four years back, marked a change in his attitude from a highly conventional thinker to a converted crusader for liberal "truth."

At age twenty-three, Gilbert had married nineteen-year-old Phyllis Miller, daughter of the housekeeper who took over when his mother died. Phyllis is a fat, complaining self-martyr who shared the bigotry of William Massey, recently deceased. During twenty years she has given Gilbert three children: two lovely blond girls, Virginia and Prudence, and a lad named Peter. They all spend much time at a house in the Blue Mountains, and when the Japanese threat to Sydney comes closer, most of the family spend most of their time at this cottage, while Glenwood is rented and Gilbert sleeps during the week either at Nick's place or that of Marty and her husband.

Gilbert finds that "he had been soberly faithful for more than twenty years to a woman he had never loved, and now heartily disliked" (159). He has an affair with Elsa Kay, who shares with him an admiration for Scott Laughlin. This affair, like most of the actions among this group during two years, is unrewarding, and its discovery by Phyllis leads her over the brink of sanity. She is, however, inept even at committing suicide, and as in earlier Dark novels, a crisis is achieved during a mountain rescue.

We share the thoughts of all these characters as they move from homes to offices to meeting places, but the effect is of a chronicle rather than a drama such as *Sun Across the Sky* or *Waterway*. And the characterization echoes the attitude of fumbling despair.

## II   *Comments on the Writer's Craft*

Gilbert's drift from conservatism to leftist leanings is not so much a pilgrimage of self-education as a rationalized revolt against his bigoted father — who was once termed by Laughlin "a hypocritical, Pharisaical, coconut-stealing, sewer-minded slum landlord because he didn't put it [his Christianity] into practice" (209). Gilbert is clearly a failure: "Parental failure had been instantly ranged in his mind beside marital failure, and failure in his one belated attempt at a love-affair; yet he found himself confronting these failures less as failures in living than as the ingredients of failure as a writer" (281). He does refrain for a while from "stealing" Elsa's idea of writing a novel based on the life of Scott Laughlin, but this ethical matter is solved when he realizes that the girl could not possibly do justice to the material.

Gilbert's sister Marty, born on January 1, 1900, does not develop during the period of the novel. She admits to being "difficult," "prickly." No one, she thinks, "could accuse me of being a pleasant person" (98). At the end of the story she begins to write a book about a downtrodden housewife. Neither does doctrinaire Nick develop, a soapbox orator at the age of thirty-five. Everyone is blighted by the dingy aspects of war on the home front, literary censorship, the discomforts and annoyances that add to the irritations of dull peacetime routine: "shatter-proofing windows, fixing blackout paper, depositing buckets of sand about the house, digging air-raid trenches, learning A.R.P. and first-aid" (169).

The most unlikable character of all is Gilbert's nagging, fat wife Phyllis, to whom he had become engaged in the throes of youthful passion during World War I, before he left to serve in France. Marty sees in Phyllis the pathos of "a human being who wanted so badly to be loved and admired — and never was; who wanted to excel, and always failed; who worshipped efficiency, deftness, brilliance, wit and learning, and who remained bungling, clumsy, dull, slow of speech, and hopelessly muddle-headed" (26). It is difficult to believe that even Gilbert could have endured Phyllis for two decades.

Phyllis is even unable to name her children properly. Virginia, pretty and flirtatious, is anything but virginal; she dies of complications caused through pregnancy by a married lover. And Prue, who badly runs an *avant-garde* bookshop, is anything but prudent, falling in love with an American soldier who departs on service.

Elsa Kay is as scrawny as a stray cat, with a white face and hollow cheeks, black hair and dark eyes, scarlet lips and "claws." She has a dry wit, but her novel had in it "the sour flavor of a grudge" (99). She is stubbornly negative, imperviously armored in egotism, and accessible only on her own terms. Others think of her as a "praying mantis." She finds Gilbert fair game for a while, but neither really likes the other.

Scott Laughlin, whose personality is supposed to haunt the two families, is a shadowy figure indeed. This mute, inglorious Fabian Socialist, who wrote poetry for the Sydney *Bulletin* and was deserted by his wife, is apparently worthy of recognition as a man who failed because he was ahead of his time; but all the reader knows of him is that he liked to help the children write better, and that he sent a humane and reproachful letter to William Massey about the family holdings in the Sydney slums. Laughlin was jailed, it was thought, during World War I as a subversive.

Among minor characters, Aunt Bee, who eloped with her lover and was cast out by her brother William, is the best rebel of the lot. Gilbert's son Peter seems to have no plot function.

*The Little Company* may not be a *roman à clef*, in which all the characters have real-life prototypes, but at least one of them resembles a person close to the author — Dr. Eric Payten Dark, who was a writer as well as a physician, and to whom this novel is dedicated. Mrs. Dark is quoted as saying: "You don't get any picture unless you have all the pieces. For example, the relation between my novels and Eric's *Medicine and the Social Order* is very clear."[5] She wrote a foreword to her husband's most controversial book, *Who Are the Reds*, which was published at the expense of the author. The conversion of Dr. Dark to the leftist cause is quite similar to that of Gilbert Massey. To continue quoting Eleanor Dark: "Eric's socialism had its genesis during the years of the depression. Previously he was completely *oblivious* to political issues. He was brought up in a strict Tory household. . . . But during the depression years Eric became more and more perturbed about the conditions of the people as he saw them exemplified in his patients and about economic factors generally. . . . The first book he brought home dealing with social conditions was Norman Angell's *Great Illusion*. From that he went from book to book till he had completed the painful process of moving from Right to Left. Oh yes! It was a very painful process."[6]

The main drawback to the success of *The Little Company* is that not one of the characters is a likable human being. Spending all the reader's time concentrating upon a selection of unhappy creatures leaves a dark-brown taste in the mouth. These are patients, not agents; the world is doing things to them, and their only response is to write down — or not write down — their irritations.

The genesis of this book is mentioned by Mrs. Dark. "Over the following three years [after 1940]," she confesses, "I wrote about another 250,000 words, different attempts at the same novel, and tore them all up. All failures. They just wouldn't go. I couldn't get any life into them. But eventually I did get onto a book, something featuring the reactions of a group of people to the war."[7]

The settings in *The Little Company* repeat those found in earlier novels — the city and the "bush." The city in this novel is not the bustling place depicted in *Waterway*. "Once so light-hearted and happy-go-lucky," Sydney had begun "to look dingy and unkempt. Under the now intolerable sunlight the parks languished, the trees wilted, the grass went straw-coloured and crackled underfoot. . . . Shop windows vanished behind boards, notices appeared saying AIR RAID SHELTER. . . . Now, robbed of its glitter . . . it was a city waiting for the sirens to wail, and its harbour reflected nothing but the stars" (176). The people "complained about raceless Sundays, they complained because there was no beer, they complained because there were no cigarettes, no houses, no matches, no mustard, no blankets, no soft drinks; they complained individually about everything; and collectively they complained with vigor and bitterness not because the burden was too heavy, but because it was not heavy enough. . . . The whole pattern of life disintegrated . . ." (204 - 5).

The gloom of the city, where Gilbert tries to improve his slum housing out of a sense of guilt, is offset somewhat by good descriptions of the Katoomba region where Eleanor Dark has spent most of her life, and bespeak her joy in bush-walking. Yet even the back country is overshadowed by Germany's attack on Russia. "He had a dim recollection now of the stony path he had followed over a high, windy tableland, of the huge valleys far below him, blue-grey, deepening to a cold purple towards late afternoon; of an eagle swooping, soaring, floating above him; of a creek where he had stopped for an icy, moss-tasting drink; but all the time he had been struggling with a new hope and a new horror" (136). Even the hills hold menace; this is "country that camouflaged its contours with dense undergrowth, enveloped you suddenly in an impenetrable veil of white mist, left you floundering, disorientated; country which quietly swallowed the inexperienced hiker and held him prisoner . . ." (154).

To the student of Eleanor Dark's development and craftsmanship, *The Little Company* may serve as the most useful text. As has been said, throughout the book are comments on authorship which are based on hard experience. These include thoughts on wartime paper shortages and censorship (62 - 63), technique (89 - 91), the chronological method of narration (121), propaganda and art (146 - 47), the tools of the writer's trade (161), and the labor of creation (289). Gilbert solves the mystery of his wife's whereabouts by drawing upon his novelist's imagination. Along with a brief article in an American magazine,[8] these comments are most enlightening about Eleanor Dark's theories concerning the writer's task.

### III  *Joyous Farewell Performance*

*The Little Company* was published in 1945, a bad year for a book about a war of which most of the world was desperately weary. Moreover, the British edition was poorly printed on cheap paper in feeble type. On the other hand, the success of *The Timeless Land* summoned reviewers to give attention to Mrs. Dark's next book, and favorable comments may have been influenced by this "halo effect."

Orville Prescott, usually a balanced critic, wrote: "Mrs. Dark writes with wit and malice and with impressive psychological penetration. Her minor characters have sharp edges and bright colors. They stand for typical human attitudes, but they do it with individual variations. . . . Mrs. Dark has made use of the petty problem of a sensitive artist upset by the violence of the world for a mature consideration of that very violence and the ethical choice it imposes on us all."[9] Praising the author's skill in evoking the Australian land, John T. Frederick wrote: "This firm earth beneath their feet is one of the reasons for the true vitality of the people of Mrs. Dark's book. They are real, not with a mere superficial accuracy of detail, but in their own natures as human beings. They have been so fully matured and integrated in the writer's mind that they become not merely like people you know — the distinction is important — but people you do know in their own right, as are the characters of all really good fiction."[10]

Virginia Sapieha was less enthusiastic. She wrote, in part: "Since the book has a thesis, and the thesis is a call to duty, it is peopled with a somewhat arbitrary cast of characters, chosen for the ideas they represent. The ties which bind them and the conflicts which sever them are more intellectual than emotional. One criterion is applied to them all, one measure by which they stand or fall — the measure of their willingness to assume responsibility for the world in which they live. . . . But neither the climax of the story nor the penetrating insight with which it is fitfully illumined are enough to integrate *The Little Company* into a moving novel."[11] In a generally unfavorable review, Jane Martin did admit: "Mrs. Dark's restless, probing curiosity, her flashes of perception, sooner or later bring to life whatever they touch. In all her human material there is a flavor of genuine native essence, illuminating to the outsider who has lazily envisaged Australia as an adjunct rather than a fiercely concentrated entity."[12]

Uther Barker, usually a champion of the author's talent, commented:

In *The Little Company* this sense of climax, of consummation after tension, is almost negative because too academically designed. Emotional crises are introduced, but the characters remain in isolation, each in his or her psychophysical void. They remain creatures of the intellect, unquickened by the breath of life. The psycho-analytical method, relentlessly applied, has pinned them down, depriving them of the power to declare themselves. . . . D. H. Lawrence once wrote 'one sheds one's sickness in books — repeats and presents again one's emotions to be master of them.' *The Little Company* might be regarded as just such a book: a spiritual discipline undertaken by the creative artist in order to escape from the toils of metaphysical facts and dedicate himself to a greater work.[13]

The most devastating comments on this novel appeared on the Red Page of the Sydney *Bulletin* in a lengthy essay on "Man and Sociology." Gilbert Massey's affair is "dolorous" and a "drama in a minor key; but at least something happens — human beings love, hate and act. It is a 'triangle'; a domestic drama; and as such is readable. A domestic drama, however, is just what Eleanor Dark has tried her hardest not to write. Gilbert's novel is to be a kind of social history in which 'Phyllis's corrosive hatred and Elsa's futile escapism' are seen as 'small things, having importance only as manifestations of a greater malaise'; and, although Gilbert is not to be identified with Eleanor Dark, it is reasonable to assume — indeed it is obvious — that *The Little Company* is an attempt to put that theory in practice." A more serious charge is that "the war is astonishingly remote in this novel. That is partly due to the rigidly Leftist propaganda Eleanor Dark submits as history." The "Red Pagan" goes on to show that the war background is skimpily and erroneously reported.[14]

The foremost critics of Australian literature give little or no space to *The Little Company*, which may be easily forgotten as a desperate effort to come to terms with a world uninterested in unpopular cerebrations. Here the novel of ideas has become the novel of propaganda, with not a gleam of humor.

Pleasant it is to recall that in Eleanor Dark's last novel, her power to portray people is given full rein and her concern for doctrines is held in check. It is almost impossible to believe that the author of *The Little Company* could also give to the world the joyous farewell performance called *Lantana Lane*.

### IV   *The Longest Shopping List*

*Lantana Lane* (1959) was a complete change from any previous type of book by Mrs. Dark, revealing an aptitude for humorous writing not suspected even by readers of the early short stories. The volume resulted from the excursion into farming by the Darks and their son from 1951 to 1957 in the Blackall Range near the coast of Queensland. The characters are imaginary neighbors on an isolated strip of land, but many of the incidents occurred as recounted, with legitimate embellishments. The structure of the book is likewise different from anything else the author had tried. Short stories and sketches are interspersed with essays — including a disquisition on that ubiquitous weed, the lantana, which takes over any unprotected inch of land and which gives its name to the winding road along which her friends lead a healthy outdoor life while trying to subsist by growing pineapples and beans and "bopplenuts."

The volume has no plot, although it holds plenty of action. Nor does it have a broad theme, unless it is that one can win health and happiness and good neighborliness on a Queensland farm but will never get rich. Some of the stories have well-made plots that would qualify them for any anthology, but the unity of the book as a whole lies in the setting. All the characters are related by proximity, and by human ties that, Mrs. Dark implies, can only be found away from the strips of asphalt that are slowly taking over Australia.

As the introductory description reveals, all the inhabitants except Jack Hawkins, whose grandfather once owned the entire southern side of the ridge, are farmers by choice rather than inheritance, and the farms vary in size from thirty-five to eight acres. The landholders are introduced, and they are a varied lot, but most of them are refugees from boring and enervating city life. Security lies in their semicommunal dependence: "We do not shut doors when we go out — far less lock them; probably the only key in the Lane is the one old Mrs. Hawkins keeps hanging on a nail in case someone's nose begins to bleed" (15 - 16). All of them suffer the curse of Eden, and labor by the sweat of their brows, "but growl and grumble as they will, the fact remains that they are farming because they want to, and they will continue to farm until they die — or (like Cain) are driven out. For let us make no mistake, driven out many of them have been, and will be" (21). Yet "it's a good life."

One of the most endearing characters, who has lived all fifty-three years of his existence in the Lane, is Herbie Bassett. For some of those years he was married to a wife devoted to interior decoration, and who drove him to weariness by a desire for gracious living that could be gratified only by winning in the state lottery. After her death Herbie devoted himself to his true vocation — staring for hours and hours at such objects as clouds and bugs and the tendrils of lantana vines. But out of habit he had continued to take out a weekly ticket on the "Casket," and when young Tommy broke the news to him that he had made a winning, he was terrified at the prospect of all the obligations a rich man would suddenly assume. He would never have time to look at things again. When it turns out that his winnings amount in all to five pounds, which will nicely cover his taxes, he is able to take it in his stride. "But he wouldn't buy no more Casket tickets; it was too risky" (36).

"The Deviation" is the first of three foreboding interchapters which describe the slow progress of the Department of Main Roads in their determination to incorporate Lantana Lane into the arterial network of the state and destroy the splendid isolation that brings comfort to its dwellers. Meanwhile, the turning into the Lane is so inconspicuous that those who ask the way are told to drive along the Tooloola-Dillillibill road "till you come to a green ute."

The story of why a vine-enshrouded utility car has become a virtually permanent landmark is the story of Joe Hardy, a taciturn bachelor who was able to drive the car on many missions (especially to play draughts with an old lady in Dillillibill on Sunday afternoons). But during a seasonal cyclone a spinning sheet of corrugated iron put him in the hospital, and Uncle Cuth became a neighborhood problem. Uncle Cuth had moved in on his nephew and literally appropriated his bed and board (his propensity for sleeping in the most comfortable bed in sight was exceeded only by his appetite for quantities of fresh-laid eggs). Since Uncle Cuth had in addition two outstanding aversions — to working and to washing — the crisis strained even the charity of the Lane's charitable hearts. Moreover, Uncle Cuth suffered from a complaint called "carbuscles." "The Lane spent much time in speculating whether these were, like corpuscles, situated internally, or like carbuncles, worn outside, but nothing was ever discovered about them except that they utterly precluded any activity whatever" (54 - 55). The ways in which noisome Uncle Cuth outstays his welcome are amusingly varied, and finally he winds up by quartering himself upon the unprotesting *voyeur* Herbie, who at the time is observing a pumpkin vine take root on the immobile green ute.

Herbie then begins shifting his attention to human beings, with fatiguing results, for he starts watching Uncle Cuth. "Herbie had not yet exhausted the wonders of the ute, and the pumpkin problem was growing every day more engrossing, and each night the stars demanded longer study, so he found Uncle Cuth almost an *embarras de richesse*, and was beginning to lose weight, and get dark circles under his eyes" (60). Just in time, Joe recovers and marches his uncle back home. Joe also discovers that his only competitor at draughts, the old lady in Dillillibill, has succumbed to a stroke, and the future looks black, until it turns out that Uncle Cuth after all is good for something — he can beat Joe at draughts most of the time. Hence the household car can still grow pumpkins, and the neighbors can still direct their friends to "just keep going till you come to a green ute."

This complete short story is followed by a brief essay on the weather in the Blackall region that should tickle the ribs of any traveler who finds that his visit anywhere has come at a time when things are "unusual." In "Quite Abnormal," it is claimed that the climate is superb — with exceptions.

Of course there was the ten-month drought a few years ago; but that was quite abnormal. . . . Nor do we have bushfires. The scrub just won't burn, and anyone who has tried to get rid of lantana by putting a match to it has learned the meaning of frustration — so it was entirely owing to the abnormal conditions that we spent most of that December racing from one farm to another, brushing breaks, and burning back as the flames kept romping up the gullies towards our pineapples. As for frosts, it is only very rarely that we see a light, silvery powder on the ground in some low-lying spot, and the time when four farms lost about twelve acres of pines between them must be regarded as the exception that proves the rule. We do cop the winds a bit, particularly the westerlies, and the northwesterlies, and the easterlies come in from the sea pretty fiercely, and the southerlies are sometimes bad, too. . . . Cyclones just have to be accepted; at least we never get them in the winter, though there was that July a few years ago when we had three — but that was quite abnormal, too. . . . Naturally one expects the wet to be wet. So we were rather shocked one year when . . . there was hardly a break in the rain from February to September. . . . It hurt our feelings to hear them [the tourists] making satirical remarks about The Sunshine State, for anyone should know that you cannot judge a climate by a spell of crazy weather. (64)

"Gwinny on Meat-day" is a full-blown sketch of Guinevere Bell, mother of a large family of children named from *Idylls of the King*. She is really the only person able to cope when her turn comes to make the weekly trip to Dillillibill to collect and deliver the community's meat, mail, and a thousand other items. Only a woman writer could think up all these items, let alone arrange them in what is probably the world's most complicated shopping list.

V *She Abjures Her Rough Magic*

"Our New Australian" is sixty-eight-year-old Mme. Isabelle Lafour, Sue Griffith's French aunt, and therefore Aunt Isabelle to all the people of Lantana Lane. She is here briefly introduced as a determined immigrant who has come to live with her niece in "the bushes" to defend her from the savages, because she has the spirit adventurous, and because she likes pineapple very much. Her adventures in traveling to Lantana Lane are deferred for a while; in this section we are introduced to her as an inveterate gossip and Gallic matchmaker, with special hopes for her friends Ken Mulliner and Elaine Bell.

Follows then the disquisition upon that botanical monster, lantana — "this dim-witted cluster of vegetation" which "zealously persists in the endless task of piling itself upon itself, and ingratiatingly adorns its gawky dishevelment with a peppering of silly little flowers" (99). Its one advantage is that it serves as a handy rubbish-dump for the neighborhood. "If Science some day passes sentence of death upon our simpleton, many strange and embarrassing sights will lie revealed" (105).

The most amusing story in the book, unless the reader happens to be unduly delicate, is "Sweet and Low." Based upon an actual happening, the tale tells how little Joy Arnold, jealous of the concentration of her friend Tony Griffith upon his new fife, siezes the instrument and either throws or drops it down that outdoor hygienic facility called the "dumpty." The retrieval scene reveals an unsuspected vein of broad comedy in the author. The poor parents are led into complicity only because Tony "was just beginning to learn 'Sweet and Low' " (117). Even the aid of Aunt Isabelle is enlisted, to boil the salvaged fife for two hours, so that the neighbors once more may enjoy the music they had almost lost — for Tony has "Sweet and Low" to perfection now, and at his father's suggestion is working on "Safely, Safely Gathered In."

Another ominous interlude on "The Deviation" results in some action by the Department of Main Roads. "With vast labor, and the expenditure of a sum which, no doubt, would have exceeded the combined annual income of the Lane, the road was actually deflected four inches to the right in one place, and six inches to the left in another, thus eliminating a curve whose existence we had not noticed until then" (125).

The next chapter views the Lane through the single eye of Nelson, the kookaburra who looks upon it as his daily source of food and amusement. This loving portrait of a specimen of Australia's "laughing jackass" bird has been anthologized. The piece demonstrates how, ever since "1788 and all that," the kookaburra, despite his raucousness and greed, has enthralled the settlers. "He must possess some necromantic art — and of course he does. He can laugh" (143). One-eyed Nelson, one of the most inimitable dwellers in the Lane, was drawn from life by a writer with two good eyes.

"The Quick Return" opens with an ironic defense of the homesteader which verges upon bitterness. "The small-scale production of sustenance — whether mental, physical, or spiritual — exposes the producer to certain subversive influences — namely, nature and solitude. These influences render him quite unfit for useful participation in the affairs of an advanced civilization, for they make him think, and wait, and stare, and dream" (141). But "there is, of course, one small problem whose solution as yet eludes us; if there were no suckers to do the primary producing, there would be nothing for the clever people to handle" (142). The sad tale of Tim and Biddy Acheson, young folk who flee "civilization" as seen from a suburban bank and go into small farming with their eyes open, reveals the details of the grim economics of the "sucker." But there is always hope, and meanwhile you grow healthy, chipping pineapples all day and living on fresh milk and beans.

"The Nuts That Were Ullaged" unravels the mystery of the disappearing "bopplenuts" that are still a neglected Queensland resource. (Taking their name from Mount Bopple in that state, these hard-shelled specimens were exported to Hawaii and grown there some years ago and now are esteemed under the name of "macadamias.") This chapter is followed by the lengthiest and in some ways the least satisfying of the stories. "The Dog of My Aunt" is an overdone account of the arrival of Aunt Isabelle in the Lane, riding in Ken Mulliner's disreputable car (named for its gameness after Ned Kelly) and accompanied by a cyclonic boxer pup named Jake. The incidents of her journey fall beyond farce, and the Frenchiness of the day's actions and diction are incompatible with the realistic traits of the rest of the Lane dwellers. Possibly Mrs. Dark had in mind her speculations on the migration of her French-bred grandmother, Eliza Howell, in the Victorian days of *Cobb et Cie.,* the Wells Fargo of Australia. But one cannot believe for very long in Aunt Isabelle.

"Serpents," on the other hand, is the story of an incident that could and did actually happen, and brought coolness for a while between Aunt Isabelle's niece, Sue Griffith, and her husband Henry.

The episode was, like "Sweet and Low," based on a next-door oc-
currence. Into the Eden of Lantana Lane come many snakes, all of
which may not molest Adam or Eve but all of which have an over-
fondness for fresh chicken. Such was the twelve-foot carpet snake
that one evening got through a hole in the netting of the fowl yard
and then, when exposed by torchlight, tried to leave by the same
door wherein he went. Sue, told to hold the two feet of writhing tail
inside the netting while Henry went to get a stick, had previously
rather defended the species Squamata. She changed her mind when
Henry could not find a weapon for what seemed like hours, and she
and the serpent in darkness were "joined together in a struggle as
fearful and implacable as man's struggle with sin" (205). The many
readers who share Sue's later disillusionment with snakes may be advised to skip this chapter.

"Bulldozed" presents a harrowing account of what happened
when Ken Mulliner decided to build a road through the lantana at
the bottom of his sloping property. The scene in which Ken decides
to guide the driver of the bulldozer through the overgrown bush and
finds himself racing for his life just ahead of the roaring monster is
witnessed by a sporting group of neighbors who cheer him on and
assess his chances of getting through an old fence and a sea of lantana.

The final story tells of the sweetly named cyclone Celestine and its
devastation of the region. Here the value of a friend in need is truly
eulogized. More overwhelming, however, is the strong community
spirit which, instead of waiting for authority to remove a fallen giant
of a tree that blocks the access of the dead-end Lane to the rest of the
world, inspires do-it-yourself action. Moreover, even a cyclone cannot diminish the sporting spirit of Lantana Lane. The effort at rescue
turns into a spirited chopping contest — north side of the Lane ver-
sus south side. Here one can leave the fascinating characters of this
Queensland Eden, not really worried that "The Deviation" will
overcome, with its mile of glassy bitumen, the investment in health
and happiness made by the indomitable small producers whose spirit
will somehow survive the "civilization" speeding past its lantana-
draped doorways.

The reviews of *Lantana Lane* were generally favorable, while expressing surprise that the author of *The Timeless Land* had after
almost two decades produced a volume showing the lightsome rather
than the serious side of her native country. "This charming and
gracefully written book can hardly fail to win the affectionate esteem

of Australian readers," began Sidney J. Baker's review.[15] Roger Covell in the Queensland *Courier Mail* agrees that "Mrs. Dark clearly knows her Queensland" and remarks that the style used for commentary "has something about it of the old-fashioned essayist," but adds: "However, if we can clear our minds of time snobbery, it is not hard to see that Mrs. Dark uses this style so well that she justifies it."[16] The Sydney *Bulletin* reviewer calls it "a book about a dream" but points out that "even Mrs. Dark — or, maybe, especially Mrs. Dark — knows it will not last."[17]

Overseas, reviewers, were equally laudatory. The London *Times Literary Supplement* contrasted farming as revealed in such widely separated regions as the Devonshire of Eden Phillpotts and the Queensland of Eleanor Dark, and remarked: "Mrs. Dark's style is by nature essayistic. She is ironical of civilization's assumptions. Her prose, delicately punctuated, but otherwise breathless, hurries us along, so that we hardly have time to reflect questioningly, 'Too many words?' Her stride, jauntily facetious in Garden-of-Eden allusions and such old stock-in-trade, suddenly finds its feet in chapters like 'The Quick Return'. . . ."[18]

The best-known critics of the Australian novel do not even mention *Lantana Lane*, but any reappraisal of Eleanor Dark's complete body of work cannot omit this "farewell tour," after which our Australian lady Prospero abjures her rough magic, breaks her staff, and drowns her book of spells.

CHAPTER 10

# The Lady and Her Career

A FTER rereading some four thousand pages of the writings of Eleanor Dark, one is entitled to ask: "Why should anyone study the works of this writer in the 1970s? What can be found of current concern in these times of questioning?"

Mrs. Dark anticipated a number of problems and answers that involve us today. She is a novelist of ideas — and many of the ideas embodied in her fiction still deserve consideration. She depicted, for example, the interrelationships of nationalism, internationalism, and imperialism. She advocated socialism long before Australia adopted a markedly socialist polity. She fought against waste — waste of land, of resources, of people. She was an advocate of the rights of black people to survive and to be respected by others. She felt strongly that, while women are the heart of the family system, they should also have lives of their own and careers to match their abilities. She believed fervently in the futility of war — and who today would challenge that doctrine? She was unpopular in some quarters because she protested against what she felt were injustices; but the wave of more violent protests in the 1960s has prepared the modern reader for outspoken, active criticism of established institutions. Use in her "psychological" novels of subjective narrative techniques such as the interior monologue infuriated some of the early reviewers who were not aware of international literary movements. For twenty years she was a leading Australian author whose every new book showed change and steady achievement, not only as a "psychological" novelist but as an "historical" novelist, and even as a writer of humorous tales about curious characters. As her most recent champion has stated, "for almost twenty years Eleanor Dark was undoubtedly the best-selling serious novelist writing in Australia."[1] She was, at the same time, widely read in Britain, continental Europe, and the United States.

## I  *Need for Solitude and Elbowroom*

Several of her qualities — some of them discussed in previous chapters — can here be mentioned in more detail. Moreover, a survey of the rise of her reputation among the critics is worthy of presentation when concluding this first volume to recognize Eleanor Dark's achievement.

Mrs. Dark's nationalism is strong. The trilogy can be read as a celebration of the separation of Australians from British ways and British domination. The first volume, in particular, makes her a forerunner of those who worked for the dismantlement of the British Empire. She is no blatant advocate of Australianity for its own sake, but love of her native land gleams from many a paragraph.

During World War II, when she was writing *The Little Company* — a book that might be read as recommending a socialist economy — she was invited to write an article on "Australia and the Australians," which voiced great hopes for her country in a time of worldwide gloom.[2] After pointing out the material accomplishments of less than a century in a land that the first settlers thought would never be able to support them, Mrs. Dark looked back to count blunders as well as achievements. "Against them must be set the ignorance and greed that used the land too recklessly, overstocking it till pastures become deserts; denuding the earth of its vegetation till the precious soil eroded, and the still more precious rivers silted up; felling trees irresponsibly, without knowledge or forethought using valuable timber for posts and rails, or even for firewood; building barbarously with no thought for beauty. And, darkest of all blunders, heaviest upon our conscience, the blunder of our dealings with the black Australians whose land we stole" (10). Herein she anticipated not only the current cry for conservation but the guilt feelings of millions who belatedly became aware of the genocide practiced against an ancient dark folk who had filled a continent with tribes living in peace in a hostile landscape.

The self-reliance of the Australian is a result, she felt, of loneliness and isolation. "Unlike many people who assert — either with complacency or irritation — that we are slavishly derivative, taking our color from England, I should say that we have evolved a variant of the English type and tradition which is quite clearly recognizable. . . . We can only say that out of as miserable and heavily handicapped a beginning as any nation ever had, and out of a handful of exiles who loathed the country, we have, in a mere century and a half, evolved a way of life which seems good to us, and bred a people to whom the country is worth dying for" (14 - 15). The national character that has developed includes humility — perhaps too much humility. "The average Australian is friendly, kind, and just. Unfortunately, being prone to define a cultured person as one who speaks the King's English, he often remains humbly unaware that in this friendliness, courtesy, and fairmindedness he himself possesses the essentials of true culture — of which ceremony, connoisseurship, and an impeccable accent are merely the sophisticated trimmings" (16).

Finally, she quotes in the article from D. H. Lawrence's *Kangaroo*: "The instinct of the place was absolutely and flatly democratic. Demos was here his own master, undisputed, and therefore quite calm about it." Eleanor Dark, during a low ebb in a world war, was able to pledge allegiance to the free nations of the globe. Her nationalism had become internationalism. "Time, which has bypassed this continent for centuries, is now hammering on our door. . . . We have felt Asia pressing down on us from above, and we have seen the Pacific shrink from an ocean to a pond. The world's business is our business; and whatever the world may require of us in the future, I think we shall be ready — on the side of Demos" (19).

Mrs. Dark's nationalism extends to an almost pantheistic love of her land. Her descriptions in the novels are matched by those in travel articles. In "They All Come Back," one result of a trip in the late 1940s that took her through all the Australian states, she depicts the "red center" of the continent and such towns as Mount Isa, Tennant Creek, and Alice Springs, whose beauty is "less of individual colors than of a color which belongs to the earth as blue belongs to the sky."[3] Even the features of an ugly mining town may have beauty — of a different sort than that of a coastal village. "They are open to a sky which roofs hundreds of miles of this gaunt, red country, and they cannot shut out the light that comes down from it. It is this necromantic light lying over the place which seems not so much to soften or excuse its defects as to transform them. Pouring down on the shabby streets, the vast mountains of slag, the stark chimneys and towering structures of a huge industrial enterprise, it uses them as a musician might use a discord to emphasize and confirm his harmony."[4] Eleanor Dark can see beauty even a thousand miles away from the wooded headlands of her Sydney Harbour.

She has been concerned also with the movement that has

nowadays come to be called "ecology." The frugality of the aborigines was repeatedly stressed in her trilogy; they lived off the land in a balanced relationship with nature, and wasted nothing of their substance. The proliferation of populations was as abhorrent to these natives as it seems to many concerned groups today. As Mrs. Dark wrote in 1951 in the same article: "But we still have other needs, not so readily recognized, among which are solitude and elbowroom. Of many available nightmare-futures, surely none could be more intolerable than a world so crowded that we could never stand upon a given spot with no other human being in sight."[5]

## II  *Integrity is Not Enough*

Eleanor Dark was an early rebel against male dominance in a country where "mum" is still often merely a part of the background. Hers was not a crude liberationism but a sturdy affirmation that women as well as men had lives to live and responsibilities to themselves. This belief did not contradict her faith in family ties and her conviction, expressed in her first published poem, that a woman's first duty is to maintain a home. Throughout the novels, however, the right of a woman to have a career and a love life is proclaimed — in the woman doctor of her first novel, *Slow Dawning*, as well as in feminine figures in its successors. A final quotation on this attitude, from a later book, expresses the feelings of the widowed Conor Mannion when she is trying to get Mark Harvey to propose to her: "Men, she reflected, by reason of their experience and wider opportunities, amassed a much greater store of knowledge than women, and their mental processes were, perhaps, more thorough — but — oh dear! — how slow! And since custom decreed that not only in matters such as this one which was now engaging their attention, but in nearly all matters, the initiative must be taken by the more slowly cerebrating half of humanity, it seemed inevitable that women should spend much of their time mentally hovering, waiting for men to catch up. . . ."[6] The germ of the celebrated trilogy, in fact, was Mrs. Dark's research for a memoir on Caroline Chisholm, a noted woman pioneer who broadened her domestic responsibilities to include seeking employment for hundreds of displaced girls and women who drifted through the streets of Sydney in the 1840s.

Mrs. Dark's advocacy of the rights of women does not rule out her admiration for male achievement. One cannot help noting, in the novels, the fact that many of her heroines are married to older men, whose judgment is often respected. In her first novel, the young woman doctor chooses a male doctor eleven years older than herself. Nigel, another wounded medico, becomes the mate of young Kay in *Prelude to Christopher*. In *Return to Coolami*, Bret is fourteen years older than Susan. Likewise, in *Waterway*, Roger Blair is fourteen years older than Lesley. In *Storm of Time*, Conor Mannion is the sixteen-year-old bride of the mature Stephen. In *The Little Company*, the girl Elsa Kay is attracted to middle-aged Gilbert Massey, and his sister Marty is married to an older man. It is no coincidence that these young women are the mates of their elders, when we recall that Eleanor Dark was married at twenty-one to a doctor more than twelve years her senior. Her admiration for older men — especially doctors, who symbolize the authority of science — is undoubtedly based on her own domestic serenity.

Eleanor Dark was a forerunner in Australia, as has been shown, in the use of the subjective method of narration. To her, thought is intellectual action, just as motion is physical action. She felt most at home in using the interior monologue — a device for which Patrick White, a fellow Australian novelist and winner of the Nobel Prize for Literature in 1973, was much later to be acclaimed. She was aware, for instance, of the celebrated passage in chapter 22 of Aldous Huxley's *Point Counterpoint* which adumbrates the psychological novel. Mrs. Dark did not follow such precepts slavishly, however; as a recent critic wrote: "While clearly aware of the development of 'the stream of consciousness,' Dark did not adopt this technique but expressed her concern with time and causation by compressing many years' memories into one or two days' action, so that we see people at a crisis point when everything that has gone before reappears to influence the outcome."[7] Chronology was an interlinking condition of human existence. Her preoccupation with time was reflected in her method: "And, crossing your own life, it held many other lives, touching, running parallel for a little while, closely woven, breaking away, so that you could never, at whatever point you chose, study a life solely your own, but always a life thrumming and alive with contacts, reacting to them in harmony or discord like the strings of a violin."[8] Later, as a rejoinder to the critics who still did not understand her intentions, Mrs. Dark inserted a comment in a novel about writers: "The writer's trick of presenting a life as the steady onward march of a personality, leaving the past behind, advancing on the future, must be, then, nothing but a lazy device to make his own task easier — a recoil of his mind from the technical intricacy of recording a man's existence as an endless present moment, moving snailwise through time, carrying the past and the future on its back."[9] She practiced, especially in the earliest novels, the less lazy device of recording intricate cerebrations with great technical skill.

Elsewhere, Mrs. Dark gave a hint in a novel concerning her method of writing. Lois, the artist in *Waterway*, is prodigal of her creative gift, and feels that any part of her experience that is needed will sooner or later emerge in her work. "She did not know . . . that it was this quality of generous extravagance, of inspired wastefulness, this capacity for spending herself recklessly, which had been, years ago, shocked by her first husband's economical storing of every thought, his anxious fear that some intricacy of plot or situation, some dexterity of phrasing might elude him and be lost for evermore" (55). In other words, a writer will not forget anything he needs to remember. Her remark might suggest that, unlike many authors, she scorns carrying a note pad day and night in the hope that a gem of action or expression will not be lost. This is, of course, a different practice than the methodical recording of notes as research for a current or future work.

The closest that Eleanor Dark came to expressing her creative creed, aside from a brief participation in a radio symposium in 1951, is found in a leading article in an American monthly magazine for people interested in writing.[10] The main purport of the article is that, while not disdaining craftsmanship, she feels that the most important quality for an aspiring writer is strong feelings about people rather than a study of techniques. The preliminary work is often done unconsciously, and "the arrangement of words, notes, forms, or colors is merely 'drawing a line around' something that already exists" (323). And "the urgency of the desire will shape the expression; the more intensely an idea has been felt, the more the writer will feel the inadequacy of his words, and the more stubbornly he will toil to overcome it." If the writer is interested in people, he will be "forced to become interested in everything else . . . in fact, in the whole world."

She states that a character in fiction cannot be the exact prototype of some real person. The novelist will "use real people less as models to be copied than as repositories upon which he can draw for a thousand different characteristics, expressions, gestures, reactions, habits, and eccentricities, any one of which is sufficient to provide the germ for an 'imaginary' character" (324). It is the quality of emotional receptivity that "makes the difference between the factual and the imaginative writer. The former has only to record — the latter has also to interpret. . . . Thus the foundation for good work in a writer is less a matter of doing than of being — and in this he is in no way peculiar. The thought from which his book will grow will depend upon the kind of person he is. And then he must 'draw a line around it.' " Finally, "the precious difference which he possesses, and which is the one thing which can give his writing character and integrity, is not to be fostered by imitation of even the most admired and illustrious giants of the literary world" (325).

This brief article cannot be taken either as an artistic credo or as advice to tyros who yearn to be published. The typical writer certainly desires strongly to be heard, but more is needed than an intense desire to put feeling into words. Certainly, a writer must observe life and respond to it, but being a person of character and integrity is not enough — he must also know how to communicate with his readers and elicit a controlled response. Eleanor Dark grew up in a literary household and unconsciously absorbed many of the attitudes and techniques of a skilled writer, and later taught herself to improve through an apprenticeship in poetry, the short story, and the novel, in which she followed many of the fashions of her time. Possibly, as a young writer, she felt that everyone knew what she knew about writing and selling magazine pieces. Her "factual" articles, such as those on biography or travel, are filled with feelings as much as are her fictions. She studied other authors of the 1920s and adapted some of their techniques for her own development. This brief article by her is thus somewhat disingenuous, and hence no further firsthand statements can be obtained that will aid the student in discerning the methods that Eleanor Dark used to create her magic in weaving a novel.

### III   *Reflections at a Golden Wedding*

In conclusion, a sampling of comments from Australian critics through the years will show the rise and growth of Eleanor Dark's literary reputation. Comments were, from the first, highly favorable. In 1937, for example, two women critics, Marjorie Barnard and Florence Eldershaw, devoted no less than sixteen pages to a discussion of Mrs. Dark's achievement, although only her first three novels were published at the time.[11] "These would seem somewhat incomplete evidence for generalization about an author still young," they wrote, "but there is substance in them and well-defined characteristics that show a clear trend. She is a successful novelist already; her work has been acclaimed" (183). After thoughtful study, they aver that "Eleanor Dark presents a world that is entirely visible and rational. Her stories are carefully constructed; every point is driven home; all that is in the minds and characters of her people is given external shape" (189).

In a survey published before the appearance of *The Timeless Land* in 1941 and designed as a guide for school reading, J. O. Anchen wrote: "The work of this author is very promising, and she shows considerable power and facility. One feels, however, that a larger canvas should be used and that more prominence should be given to the brighter side of life."[12] The larger canvas was being painted at the time, but not all the moods were to be bright.

The acclaim given *The Timeless Land* in Australia and overseas, noted in chapters 6 and 8, established Eleanor Dark as one of the foremost writers of her country. As one reviewer agreed, "Eleanor Dark is one of those lucky writers who, in their lifetime, achieve success while feeling reasonably sure of a permanent place in their national literature. . . . When posterity comes to examine our writing record, she will have to rank as one of the twentieth-century Australian writers who meant something."[13] A critic interested in history proclaimed that Australian prose was sadly lacking in social criticism, but that in *The Timeless Land* it found strong expression. "This novel of Mrs. Dark's is perhaps the most distinguished of the few serious works of art that have entered the Australian literary scene. I place it in the category of Wells's *Tono Bungay*, Koestler's *Darkness at Noon*, and Huxley's *Brave New World*. Love, hate, and jealousy, murder and envy, have formed the staple of many thousands of novels, but these four books moved away from the microcosm of the individual into the macrocosm of the world. They depict the forces at work in the milieu of man determining his destiny."[14]

A survey of the novels in 1950 began: "By present standards Eleanor Dark is the most distinguished living Australian woman novelist, but she is essentially a daughter of her generation. Whether her quality will endure posterity can decide for itself. Certainly she has the ability possessed by all great creative writers of leading the reader into a world like, yet unlike, the everyday one — a new world created and peopled by its author's imagination. Eleanor Dark's imagination is so intense, she is such a consummate storyteller, that she can make incredible circumstances real."[15] A few months later, in a critique by a personal friend, the novelist's originality is stressed.

Eleanor Dark is essentially individual in thought and expression, and it would be profitless to attempt to compare her with any other writer living or dead. I can trace in her work no direct influence of earlier or contemporary writers, though undoubtedly she has gained much from wide and intelligent reading. Her concern, it seems, has been more with the gathering of historic facts than ways of presenting them; with the many and varied creations of character, and the interplay of minds, rather than the technique of the creator. Her debt is to Life itself, and she is repaying it with honesty and generous purpose. Honesty is the keynote of her writing, a stubborn integrity that no promise of easy popularity can shake; it controls the most emotional passages, and gives to her work authority and character.[16]

Professor G. A. Wilkes, in a scholarly article on Mrs. Dark's development, is often captious, but acknowledges that, "while the contrast between the early work and the later is emphatic, the movement from one novel to the next has been fluid: Eleanor Dark has developed by making each successive book 'include' the one before it. Though some of her work is therefore repetitive, it nevertheless exhibits continuity and pattern — a pattern which has not yet, of course, been completed."[17] A decade later, the foremost Australian literary critic devoted no less than eleven large pages to the work of Eleanor Dark, beginning with the declaration that

Mrs. Dark and a few others have proved that there are now readers for novels whose atmosphere and characters are at once Australian and those of a wider world: the types represented by her characters and at least a considerable proportion of her readers are in an even smaller minority in Australia than elsewhere, but they do exist and are at the same time rooted in their own country. What is more, they are emotionally as well as intellectually awake; Mrs. Dark may be described as an intellectual romantic, for whom the worlds of thought and feeling are equally important: broadly speaking, that is, for while in her earlier novels emotion predominates, in the later novels reflection gains upon it, though neither is ever without elements of the other; as with the typical poet, her emotions are intellectualized, and at the same time her ideas are felt in the blood. And in her principal characters there is the struggle between mind and emotion, so far as these can be regarded separately: a struggle that is often intense, so that in her novels generally, but more especially in the earlier novels, we are conscious of a sometimes almost unbearable strain.[18]

And finally, in a broad survey of Australian fiction since 1920, Professor Harry Heseltine concludes that the novels of Eleanor Dark seem to be much less the result of spontaneous delight in people and places than the conscious exploration of the possibilities of fiction. Perhaps for this reason her work exemplifies with remarkable thoroughness nearly all the vital interests which animated the Australian novel in the years which preceded the Second World War. . . . There is a considered ingenuity about the construction of *Prelude to Christopher*. There is a similar sophistication of technique in *Return to Coolami*. . . . The novel bears witness, like all of Dark's earlier work, to a thorough schooling in the techniques of modern fiction. Her works exhibit the virtues of a well-trained and well-stored intelligence applying itself to 'he task of creating literature. During the thirties, Dark's conception of her task seems to have undergone some change. Certainly, *The Timeless Land*, which appeared in 1941, manifests a distinct shift from the themes of personal conflict and depth psychology which dominated the earlier books. . . . It is documented with a truly impressive accumulation of historical detail. There is a heroic vision of a nation begun in the most adverse conditions yet sustained by the unswerving purpose of its first governor, Captain Arthur Phillip. There is the kaleidoscope of all the elements of the miniscule society. And there is the imagined life of the aborigines, who had come to terms with the land generations before the arrival of the First Fleet.[19]

In 1972, when the Darks celebrated their golden wedding anniversary at their Katoomba home, they might have reflected comfortably that Eleanor's career as one of the foremost Australian writers of fiction was engraved upon the annals of her beloved land.

# Notes and References

## Chapter One

1. Eric Lowe, *Book News* 1 (Sept. 1946), 81.
2. Mrs. Dark and her brother remember a legend that a passage had been booked to Australia for the Howell family, but by some accident the ship sailed without them and they had to travel by the next one. The ship they missed was the celebrated *Dunbar*, wrecked in The Gap just outside Sydney Heads in 1857, with only one survivor.
3. A tablet in St. Philip's reads: "In memory of the Rev. Thomas O'Reilly, for twelve years Incumbent of this Church and Canon of St. Andrew's Cathedral. Died Dec. 18, 1881. A Beloved brother and a faithful Minister. Eph. VI-21."
4. *The Prose and Verse of Dowell O'Reilly* (Sydney, 1924), with preface by D.G.F.
5. E. Morris Miller in his usually impeccable two-volume pioneer work, *Australian Literature* (Melbourne, 1940), lists a nonexistent Dark novel, *White Fire* (1937). This confusion probably resulted because at one time this title was considered for *Sun Across the Sky*.
6. Harry Heseltine, "Australian Fiction Since 1920," in *The Literature of Australia*, ed. Geoffrey Dutton (Adelaide: Penguin Books, 1964), pp. 205 - 206.
7. Jean Devanny, *Bird of Paradise* (Sydney, 1945), pp. 247 - 48.
8. Eric Lowe, "Eleanor Dark," *Walkabout* 17 (May 1, 1951), 8.
9. "The Blackall Range Country," *Walkabout* 21 (Nov. 1, 1955), 18 - 20.

## Chapter Two

1. *Triad* 6 (June 10, 1921), 27.
2. Devanny, *Bird of Paradise* (Sydney, 1945), p. 248. Mrs. Dark once remarked to me: "I especially liked the fee received for a sonnet. It exactly paid for a bag of fertilizer for my garden!"
3. A rather slight piece, "The Desire of the Moth," about a parish spinster and her first kiss, appeared in the Christmas, 1924, issue of *Art in Australia* under the pseudonym of "Henry Head."
4. *Bulletin*, (Sydney), Dec. 12, 1925, p. 44.
5. *Australia* 2 (March, 1946), 19.

6. Ibid., p. 20.

7. Speaking to an interviewer about the writing of *Slow Dawning*, Mrs. Dark said: "That was the only time in my life when I wrote dishonestly, deliberately wrote down with the object of making money. I regard it as a judgment upon me that it was not published till many years later, in 1932, which meant that what money I did make out of it — and it did as well as I expected — I did not get at the time I wanted it. I think that writing with the tongue in the cheek is asking for trouble. From every point of view it is a bad policy." Devanny, *Bird of Paradise*, p. 248.

8. Hereafter, to avoid excessive footnoting, page numbers of references to a novel appear in the text in parentheses after a passage quoted.

9. G. A. Wilkes, "The Progress of Eleanor Dark," *Southerly*, 2 (1951), 140.

10. Eric Lowe, *Book News* 1 (Sept., 1946), 79.

11. H. M. Green, *A History of Australian Literature* (Sydney, 1961), II, 1079. (Hereafter, this work is referred to as Green, *A History . . .*)

## Chapter Three

1. Page numbers in parentheses refer to the Rigby softbound edition of *Prelude to Christopher*.

2. Devanny, *Bird of Paradise* (Sydney, 1945), p. 254.

3. Ibid., pp. 251-52.

4. Eric Lowe, *Book News* 1 (Sept., 1946), 81.

5. "G.M.M.," "A Novelist at Home," *Morning Herald* (Sydney), May 23, 1935, Women's Supplement, p. 17. A contradiction appears in this comment. The novelist who spends a year thinking about a book can hardly be accused of not planning. The structure of *Prelude to Christopher* is tight and controlled, not at all damaged by the behavior of a character who runs away with the plot.

6. "Our Writers, VIII: Eleanor Dark," *Overland*, no. 15 July, 1959), p. 39.

7. "R.P.," "Several Novels by Women," *Bulletin*, April 22, 1936, p. 4.

8. "These events are not communicated directly to the reader but through what purport to be the reflections of the characters. The ruse is common enough in novels, but is rarely carried so far as in *Sun Across the Sky*, where the effect, besides slowing the action appreciably, is to postulate several characters with equal introspective powers exercising them at great length and on the same day with extraordinary aptness to the author's need — a not very natural proceeding." Anon, "Eleanor Dark's New Novel," *Bulletin* 58 (Sept. 22, 1937), 8.

9. Devanny, *Bird of Paradise*, p. 254.

10. "The Progress of Eleanor Dark," *Southerly*, no. 3 (1951), p. 140.

11. *All About Books* 7 (June 12, 1934), 115.

12. *Book News* 1 (Sept., 1946), 79.

13. "A Eugenic Tragedy," Nov. 5, 1936.

## Chapter Four

1. Page numbers in parentheses in this chapter refer to the hardbound editions of *Return to Coolami* (published by Collins and identical with the Fontana softbound edition) and *Sun Across the Sky* (Macmillan).

2. *Book News* 1 (Sept., 1946), 81.

3. "R.P.," "Several Novels by Women," *Bulletin*, April 22, 1936, pp. 2 - 4.

4. "A.C.," "Fiction," *Saturday Review of Literature* 14 (June 20, 1936), 19.

5. "Australian Journey," *New York Times Book Review*, June 14, 1936, p. 16.

6. Sarah T. Dickson, "Discovery of Contentment in Australia," *New York Herald-Tribune Books*, June 14, 1936, p. 8.

7. "An Australian Story," *Morning Herald*, Feb. 21, 1936, p. 7.

8. T. Inglis Moore, *Social Patterns in Australian Literature* (Sydney, 1971), p. 300.

9. *The Penguin Book of Modern Australian Verse*, ed. R. G. Howarth, Kenneth Slessor, and John Thompson (London, 1958), p. 25.

10. "Eleanor Dark's Novels," *All About Books* 9 (Oct. 12, 1937), 150.

11. "Novels of the Day," *Morning Herald* (Sydney), Sept. 24, 1937, p. 7.

12. "Eleanor Dark's New Novel," *Bulletin* (Sydney), Sept. 22, 1937, p. 8.

13. Louise M. Field, "A Pair of Geniuses," *New York Times Book Review*, Nov. 14, 1937, p. 7.

14. Lorine Pruette, "Sun Across the Sky," *New York Herald-Tribune, Books*, Oct. 31, 1937, pp. 10, 14.

15. Cecil Hadgraft, *Australian Literature: A Critical Account* (London, 1960), p. 235.

## Chapter Five

1. Page numbers in parentheses in this chapter refer to the hardbound edition of *Waterway*, published by Collins.

2. "The Progress of Eleanor Dark," *Southerly*, no. 3 (1951), p. 143.

3. Ibid., pp. 143 - 44.

4. "This constant employment of accident as a *deus ex machina* has been labeled melodramatic, but I suspect that it is probably a form of realism coming naturally to the wife of a doctor who may be concerned with accidental death and injury day by day. On the other hand, I feel that there is little somberness of fatalism, little sense of man as victim, since the accident seems created, not by fate, but by the firm shaping hand of Eleanor Dark as the skillful craftsman." T. Inglis Moore, *Social Patterns in Australian Literature* (Sydney, 1971), pp. 154 - 55.

5. The ferry *Greycliffe* was struck astern by R.M.S. *Tahiti* — a Union Steamship liner bound for San Francisco — about 4:30 on the afternoon of Thursday, November 3, 1927, off Bradley's Head. Although other vessels

soon came to the aid of the struggling passengers, more than forty persons were dead or missing, and fifty were hospitalized. Most of the deaths were caused by drowning. See Sydney *Morning Herald*, Nov. 4, 1927, pp. 13, 14; Nov. 7, p. 11; Nov. 10, p. 11; Nov. 12, p. 17; and Nov. 14, p. 11.

6. "Art and Accident," *Bulletin*, March 5, 1947, 2.

7. Eleanor O'Reilly's mother died on August 6, 1914.

8. Wilkes (pp. 142 - 43) observes with some harshness: "Roger Blair . . . is in *Waterway* regarded by Mrs. Dark with a special affection. But as she never convincingly *demonstrates* Blair's superior qualities, he leaves the impression of sounding brass and tinkling cymbal. As Blair is preferred by Lesley Channon, we perforce revise our estimate of Lesley's intelligence, and her character goes awry. There is a cleavage between intention and performance. That it is not due to the social theme alone is apparent from the instance of Lois, who in Mrs. Dark's estimation is a spirit of a rare order, and who on Mrs. Dark's showing has less intelligence than is usually necessary to support life." This may be contrasted with the opinion of H. M. Green, the standard historian of Australian literature: "Among the best drawn of all Mrs. Dark's characters, principal or minor, is Lois, in *Sun Across the Sky* and *Waterway*, a fascinating study of a certain variety of the artistic temperament, and yet thoroughly individualized and lifelike: simple, even naive, and outside her work quite helpless but in her work a master; warm and human and entirely natural; almost as good, so far as it goes, is the glimpse we get of her daughter Chloe." Green, *A History* . . . (Sydney, 1961), II, 1081. Green also has high praise for Mrs. Dark's powers of external description in all her novels — in illustration, he quotes two passages from the scene of the ferry wreck in *Waterway*.

9. "Novels of the Day: A Sydney Day," *Morning Herald*, June 24, 1938, p. 6. In a letter to a friend, speaking of the reviewer's comment that she was "too omnipotent," Mrs. Dark wrote: "If this means anything at all it means that the reviewer believes that the author can 'make' his characters do anything he likes, which, as you know, is just plain blasphemy to me! . . . The queerest instance of all was Lois. I simply forgot all about her. When the accident was over, and the passengers struggling in the water, I suddenly thought: 'Good heavens, what happened to Lois?' She wasn't on board! . . . I realized that sitting in the sun she had, as usual, gone to sleep — and because her own consciousness had ceased *pro tem*, my consciousness of her had also logically and inevitably ceased." Again this author seems disingenuous. She had "planted" this possibility as early as page 51 of the novel, speaking of Lois: "Her capacity for sleep was astonishing. Not only at night, but at odd times during the day she slept." Concern about the fate of Lois adds to suspense after the crisis. Eleanor Dark was never a victim of her characters. The plotting in *Waterway* is so well planned that it verges upon slickness.

10. "A Dramatic Novel of Australia," *New York Times Book Review*, Aug. 7, 1936, p. 6.

11. "Twenty-four Hours in the Antipodes," *Saturday Review of Literature* 18 (Aug. 13, 1938), p. 6.

12. "Waterway," *New York Herald-Tribune*, Aug. 14, 1938, pp. 7 - 8.

13. "A Local Novel Comes Home," *Daily Telegraph* (Sydney), Feb. 22, 1947.

14. *Australian Literature: A Critical Account* (London, 1960), p. 235.

15. *Introduction to Australian Fiction* (Sydney, 1950), pp. 142 - 43.

## Chapter Six

1. "Caroline Chisholm and Her Times," in *The Peaceful Army: A Memorial to the Pioneer Women of Australia*, ed. Flora S. Eldershaw (Sydney, 1938), pp. 59 - 84.
After giving some background data on nineteenth-century Sydney, the convict population first settling there in 1788, the aborigines of the region, the emigrants, and the role of religion, Mrs. Dark embarks on a fine portrait of Mrs. Chisholm, whose story is well known but cannot be retold too often. The key word throughout the article is "family." Mrs. Chisholm, although having a husband and three children of her own at her home in Windsor, at some distance from Sydney, was impelled by the plight of homeless people in the city to beard gruff Governor Gipps and demand forty-nine square feet of space in an abandoned, rat-ridden public building in which she could open a center for desperate females adrift in the city. "There were, in 1841, six hundred respectable women unemployed in Sydney. Young girls of good character roamed the streets by day and slept under the rocks in the Domain at night" (p. 69). As a child, Mrs. Chisholm's favorite game was ferrying doll families across the sea of a wash-basin. Not only a reformer but "a female reformer in an age when fearless thinking and independent action were not generally considered desirable, or even quite respectable, attributes" (p. 60), she arranged, during seven years of hard work, to find employment for no less than eleven thousand persons around the countryside, often leading a group from farm to farm, seated on an ox cart. She arranged contracts with good families for hired girls, who often married and founded families. When Mrs. Chisholm decided that she would have to go to England to fight the lazy government, to send left-behind children to join their overseas families, and to reform the whole system of emigration, she did so and founded a Family Colonisation Loan Society, which in the two years from 1850 to 1852 sent out seven shiploads of selected emigrants to start new families in New South Wales. Even when the discovery of gold in 1854 brought a flood of new souls to Australia and she was able to return to her family, she criticized the lack of family life at the diggings and tried to make land available for homesteading. As Mrs. Dark points out, "She looked to the completed structure of a nation, but was content to lay its foundations faithfully, man by man, woman by woman, child by child, seeing in the *united family* the nucleus, the essential life-cell of progress" (p. 60). Caroline Chisholm was

truly one of the greatest of Australian women, and "the story of her work is still going on in hundreds of Australian homes." Eleanor Dark's own devotion to family made her an especially qualified biographer of such an early heroine.

2. *Waterway* (Sydney, 1938), pp. 216 - 19.

3. Devanny, *Bird of Paradise*, p. 252. The article on Bennelong (*sic*) in the *Australian Encyclopedia* (Sydney, 1965) states that in 1788 this native was about twenty-six years old and was killed in January, 1813, in a tribal fight.

4. The authenticity of her treatment of aboriginal ethnology is vouched for by Dr. A. P. Elkin, formerly Professor of Anthropology at the University of Sydney, according to H. M. Green, *A History* . . . II, p. 1093. Mrs. Dark acknowledges as sources the works not only of Professor Elkin but of Dr. Herbert Basedow, Dr. Phyllis Kaberry, Dame Mary Gilmore, and Mrs. Daisy Bates, C.B.E. (note that the latter three are women). Concerning her use of contemporary journals, letters, and official documents in order to portray the period, one critic states: "I can only detect one mistake of fact among the thousands refered to in the three novels." Stephen Murray-Smith, "Darkness at Dawn," *Australian Book Review* 2 (Sept., 1963), 178.

5. Page numbers in parentheses in this chapter refer to the 1965 (reset) edition of *The Timeless Land*, which is more readily available than the first editions of 1941, British and American.

6. Humphrey McQueen, "The Novels of Eleanor Dark," *Hemisphere* (Canberra) 17 (Jan., 1973), 41.

7. See, for example, Dr. John Cobley, *Sydney Cove 1778: The First Year of Settlement in Australia* (London, 1962); *Sydney Cove 1789 - 90* (Sydney, 1963); and *Sydney Cove 1791 - 92* (Sydney, 1965).

8. Stephen Murray-Smith, "Darkness at Dawn," *Australian Book Review* 2 (Sept., 1963), 178.

9. *Introduction to Australian Fiction* (Sydney, 1950), p. 143.

10. Cecil Hadgraft, *Australian Literature* (London, 1960), p. 236.

11. G. A. Wilkes, "The Progress of Eleanor Dark," *Southerly*, no. 3 (1951), p. 145.

12. John McKellar, "The Black and the White," *Southerly* 9 no. 2 (1948), 94.

13. Ibid., p. 98.

14. Donald Horne, *The Next Australia* (Sydney, 1971), pp. 117 - 18.

15. Green, *A History* . . . , II, p. 1093.

16. One gets a first impression that a good deal of the novel consists of quoted documents. Actually, these passages — helpfully printed in italics — are not extremely frequent; some letters in italics, like those of Stephen Mannion, are from imaginary characters. However, Mrs. Dark did much reading and took hundreds of notes from manuscript sources and collections like *Historical Records of New South Wales* (Sydney, 1892) and *Historical*

*Records of Australia* (Sydney, 1914). To help the author in her portrayal of the governor she had available *Admiral Arthur Phillip* (Sydney, 1937), by Dr. George Mackaness. The Mitchell Library in Sydney contains voluminous manuscripts by Phillip, Hunter, Tench, White, and other early writers.

17. A novel about the Bryants, *A First Fleet Family* by Louis Becke, appeared in London in 1896. Nonfiction accounts include *The Strange Case of Mary Bryant* by Geoffrey Rawson (London, 1938) and *Boswell and the Girl from Botany Bay* by Frederick A. Pottle (New York, 1937).

18. "Though it may have been envisaged as the story of Bennilong, its true protagonist — as more than one has noted — is the timeless land itself." G. A. Wilkes, "Progress of Eleanor Dark," 145.

19. Green, *A History* . . . , II, p. 1094.

20. "It Happened in Australia," 24 (Oct. 4, 1941), 5.

21. "Out of Australia," Oct. 4, 1941, p. 316.

22. Oct. 5, 1941, pp. 5, 18.

23. "Birth of a Nation — Down in Australia," Oct. 5, 1941, p. 5.

24. "Novels of the Week: Redemption," Nov. 1, 1941, p. 541.

25. "Terra Incognita," Dec. 20, 1941, p. 8.

26. "Two Historical Novels," Jan. 7, 1942, p. 2.

27. "Matrix of the Past," *B.P. Magazine*, June 1, 1942, p. 62.

28. McKellar, "Black and White," p. 98.

29. "Two Australian Novelists Interpretations of Early History," *Victorian Historical Magazine* 26 (Dec., 1954), 57.

30. Green, *A History* . . . , II, p. 1096.

31. In *The Pattern of Australian Culture* (Ithaca, N.Y., 1963), p. 87.

32. In *The Literature of Australia* (Adelaide, 1964), p. 199.

## Chapter Seven

1. Page references in parentheses in this chapter refer to pagination in the hardbound first edition of *Storm of Time* (London-Sydney, 1948). The 1963 reprint has the same pagination as the first edition.

2. Much of Book III is a dramatization of the historical events. For nonfiction accounts see, for example, *The Life of Vice-Admiral William Bligh, R.N.* (Sydney, 1951, 1956), by George Mackaness, and *John Macarthur* (Sydney, 1955), by M. H. Ellis.

3. "L.V.K.," "Non-Fiction," Oct. 30, 1948, p. 6.

4. Nov. 10, 1948, p. 2.

5. Dorothy Cubis, *Journal of the Royal Australian Historical Society* 35 (1949), 65.

6. No. 2, 1950, p. 101.

7. Ulrich B. Davis, "When Bligh of the *Bounty* Ruled Australia," *New York Herald-Tribune Books*, Jan. 29, 1950, p. 19.

8. Nash K. Burger, "Old Australia," Feb. 5, 1950, p. 30.

9. Winifred King Rugg, "Phrased with Grave Beauty," Feb. 9, 1950, p. 15.

10. Victor P. Haas, "Bligh of Botany Bay," 30 (Feb. 25, 1950), 19.

## Chapter Eight

1. Page references in parentheses in this chapter refer to pagination in the hardbound first edition of *No Barrier* (London-Sydney, 1954). The 1963 reprint has the same pagination as the first edition.

2. The difficulties of crossing the mountains were excellently explained to the writer by Mrs. Dark in a letter of June 26, 1965. "This [early] expedition was made by Dawes, Johnston and Lowes with a few marines — Tench was not with them; he and Collins both described it from hearsay in their books. Collins says that Dawes' line of march unfortunately and unpleasantly for him, happened to lie . . . across a line of high, steep, rocky precipices which required much caution in descending and much labour in ascending.' This is a very just description, and illustrates the reason why expeditions were unsuccessful for so long. The mountains are rough like the backbone of a fish — one main ridge, and many subsidiary ones leading off it on either side; early parties tried to walk across the subsidiary ridges instead of following the main one (as Blaxland, Wentworth, and Lawson eventually did), and consequently they were always climbing in and out of gullies that became deeper as the mountains became higher. The gully walls were still scalable beyond where Dawes & Co. stopped — we have scaled them ourselves, and without any real climbing (i.e. necessitating ropes), but finding ways up and down them would have taken a long time, and they had no food except what they carried. Aborigines could 'live off the land,' but even they wouldn't have found much in that region."

3. "When Macquarie Ruled," June 20, 1953.

4. "The Great Australian Novel?" July 11, 1953, p. 8.

5. Murray Tonkin, "Beyond the Mountains a New Land," July 12, 1953.

6. "Three Australian Novels," July 15, 1953, p. 2.

7. A. G. L. Shaw, 12, no. 3 (1953), 342 - 43.

8. "A Very Human Villain," *A.M.*, Feb. 16, 1954.

9. "*No Barrier* Falls Short," June 28, 1953, p. 17.

10. *Bulletin*, July 11, 1953, p. 8.

11. "Three Australian Novels," ibid., p .2

12. Nancy Keesing, ibid., Aug. 24, 1953, p. 42.

13. John McKellar, "Two Australian Novelists' Interpretations of Early History," *Victorian Historical Magazine* 26 (Dec., 1954), 57.

14. *Australian Literature* (London, 1960), p. 238.

15. Stephen Murray-Smith, "Darkness at Dawn," *Australian Book Review* 2 (Sept., 1963), 178.

16. Humphrey McQueen, "The Novels of Eleanor Dark," *Hemisphere* (Canberra) 17 (Jan., 1973), 38.

## Chapter Nine

1. Page numbers in parentheses in this chapter refer to the Collins edition of *The Little Company* and the hardbound Collins edition of *Lantana Lane*.

2. *Bulletin*, July 11, 1945, p. 2.

3. *Australian Literature: A Critical Account* (London, 1960), p. 235.

4. David Low, born in 1891 in New Zealand, was on the staff of the Sydney *Bulletin* in 1911 and on the staff of the London *Star* in 1919; he was a famed political cartoonist and created the character of Colonel Blimp.

5. Devanny, *Bird of Paradise*, p. 251.

6. Ibid., pp. 253 - 54. Dr. Dark, born at Mittagong, N.S.W., on June 23, 1889, attended Sydney Grammar School and earned the degree of M.D. from the University of Sydney. He published his first book, *Diathermy in General Practice*, in 1929. *Medicine and the Social Order* (1942), with an epigraph quoting Eugene Debs, an American Socialist leader, opens with three chapters originally appearing in the *Medical Journal of Australia* in 1937, 1939, and 1941. In his preface Dr. Dark says, in part: "So, without any deliberate design on my part, but simply as the result of following to their logical conclusion the facts as I found them, the book has become an indictment of capitalism, and a plea for socialism as the only alternative to a recoil into a darker age than the world has ever seen." The book is dedicated to his wife. The essays contain factual and often quite sensible comments on malnutrition, unemployment, war, property, housing, crime and prisons, Marxist economics, education, and the achievements of the Soviet Union. However, these comments hardly justify such a "conclusion" as: "It is essential that all who are capable of thought should now decide finally in which camp they belong — the fascist, or the socialist. . . . A neutral position is impossible, because, as we have seen, Fascism is the natural end of monopoly capitalism. Those who do not wish that end to be reached must take an active part in wrenching capitalism from its natural road, and turning it to socialism. Everyone who remains passive is an ally, conscious or unconscious, of the Fascists." Such a drastic example of the "either/or" fallacy, of course, might be pardoned in the middle of a world war.

Publication of *Who Are the Reds* (1946) was less well advised. The essays, written from January through March, 1945, attempt to support the premise that "Reds" are always reformers who are rejected by society. Three chapters describe the radical acts of Christ, the Gracchi, and Sacco and Vanzetti. Three others describe the benefits of Communist activity in China, Yugoslavia, and Greece. The final chapter claims that in Australia, liberal thinkers are smeared as "Communists." Dr. Dark therein says he is not a member of the Communist Party but has many Communist friends and acquaintances. "Knowing these men and women as well as I do I see the best of them (they vary in quality like all groups) as the modern counterparts of the early Christians" (p. 105). A foreword by Eleanor Dark says, in part: "It is the business of those who have convictions to express them; they will be rejected or endorsed, in an immediate sense, by the contemporary world, and in the last resort by posterity. Thus we face a challenge in our attempts to analyse the contemporary convictions which are expressed to us. . . . This pamphlet expresses a conviction. As the wife of its author I am in a position to know that it is not an irresponsible one; that it has been hardly, and even unwillingly, gained during years of study and research; that it has literally forced itself upon a mind which gave it no other encouragement than to hold open, stubbornly, the door of intellectual honesty." Dr. Dark's views deserve the same consideration as those expressed by Gilbert Massey in *The Little Company.*

7. Devanny, *Bird of Paradise*, p. 252.

8. "Drawing a Line Around It," *Writer* (U.S.) 59 (Oct., 1946), 323.

9. "The Little Company," *New York Times*, May 9, 1945, p. 21.

10. "I've Been Reading," *Sun* (Chicago), May 13, 1945.

11. "The Little Company," *New York Herald-Tribune Review of Books*, May 13, 1945, p. 6.

12. "The Little Company," *New York Times Books*, May 20, 1945, pp. 16 - 17.

13. "The Little Company," *Meanjin Papers*, no. 2 (1946) p. 167.

14. "Man and Sociology," July 11, 1945, p. 2. However, Geoffrey Serle in *From Deserts the Prophets Come* (Melbourne, 1973), classes *The Little Company* as "among the first significant novels of ideas in Australian writing."

15. "Our Good Earth," *Morning Herald*, May 23, 1959.

16. "Eleanor Dark Turns Out a Good One," May 9, 1959.

17. "Happy Families," June 24, 1959, p. 2.

18. "Salt of the Earth," April 10, 1959.

## Chapter Ten

1. Humphrey McQueen, "The Novels of Eleanor Dark," *Hemisphere* (Canberra) 17 (Jan., 1973), 38.

2. *Australia Week-end Book* #3 (Sydney, 1944), pp. 9 - 19.

3. *Walkabout* 17 (Jan. 1, 1951), 19 - 20.

4. Ibid., p. 19.

5. Ibid., p. 20.

6. *No Barrier*, p. 91.

7. McQueen, p. 38.

8. *Waterway*, p. 13.

9. *The Little Company*, p. 121.

10. *The Writer* 59 (Oct., 1946), 323 - 25.

11m''m.abua/ a/d Eldershaw,'Essays in Australian Fiction (Melbourne, 1938), pp. 182 - 98.

12. *The Australian Novel: a Critical Survey* (Melbourne and Sydney, n.d.), p. 32.

13. "Miss Bronte," "Torture Step by Step," *Telegraph* (Sydney), July 14, 1945, p. 13.

14. John McKellar, "The Black and the White," *Southerly* 9, no. 2 (1948), 92.

15. Margaret Kiddle, "The Novels of Eleanor Dark," *Week End Review* 1 (Nov. 17, 1950), 259.

16. Eric Lowe, "The Novels of Eleanor Dark," *Meanjin* 10, no. 4 (1951), 341.

17. "The Progress of Eleanor Dark," *Southerly*, no. 3 (1951), p. 139.

18. H. M. Green, *A History* . . . , II, pp. 1077 - 78.

19. "Australian Fiction Since 1920," in *The Literature of Australia* (Adelaide, 1964), pp. 198 - 99.

15. Green, *A History* . . . , II, p. 1093.

# Selected Bibliography

No book about Eleanor Dark exists, other than the present one, nor has a complete bibliography ever been published. It has thus seemed wise to make this section as complete as possible, even at the risk of including pseudonymous poems and short stories and casual pieces, while this material is still recoverable. A "Handlist of Eleanor Dark's Books and Critical References" was published in *Biblionews* (Sydney) for August, 1954, by Hugh Anderson of Apollo Bay, Victoria, and I here acknowledge his additional aid in checking items accumulated over many years in his files.

The items below are given chronologically, except for "Other Sources," which are given alphabetically by author. Some Australian periodicals do not use volume numbers.

PRIMARY SOURCES

1. Books

*Slow Dawning.* London: John Lane, Ltd. [1932], 288 pp.

*Prelude to Christopher.* Sydney and Melbourne: P. R. Stephensen & Co., 1934, 317 pp.; London: Collins, 1936; Leipzig: Tauchnitz, 1937 (softbound); Adelaide: Rigby, Ltd., 1961 (softbound).

*Return to Coolami.* London: Collins, 1936, 319 pp.; New York: Macmillan, 1936; Australia White Circle Pocket Novel Series, n.d.; London: Fontana Books, 1961 (softbound).

*Sun Across the Sky.* London: Collins, 1937, 336 pp.; New York: Macmillan, 1937; Leipzig: Tauchnitz, 1938 (softbound); Australia White Circle Pocket Novel Series, n.d.; *Il Sole Nel Cielo* (Italian trans.), Verona: Arnoldo Mondadore Editore, 1948 (softbound); *Le Faiseur d' Étoiles* (French trans.), Paris: Hachette, 1948 (softbound).

*Waterway.* London: Collins, 1938, 445 pp.; New York: Macmillan, 1938; Sydney: F. H. Johnson, 1946.

*The Timeless Land.* London and Sydney: Collins, 1941, 447 pp.; New York: Macmillan, 1941; Sydney: Collins, 1963. The 1963 edition omits the Bibliography, as does the New York edition. *Der erste Gouverneur* (German trans.), Hannover: Adolf Sponholtz, 1954 (abridged);

*Tidlöst Land* (Swedish trans.), Stockholm, 1945 (softbound). Other softbound editions, in English, include Penrith, N.S.W.: Discovery Press, 1972 (Modern Australian Library) and London: Collins, 1973 (Fontana Books).

*The Little Company.* Sydney and Auckland: Collins, 1945, 318 pp.; New York, Macmillan, 1945.

*Storm of Time.* London and Sydney: Collins, 1948, 590 pp.; New York, McGraw-Hill Book Co., 1950 (introduction by Allan Nevins); Sydney: Collins, 1963.

*No Barrier.* London and Sydney: Collins, 1953, 384 pp.; Sydney: Collins, 1963.

*Lantana Lane.* London: Collins, 1959, 254 pp.; Humorbooks, Sydney Ure Smith and London: Horwitz Group Books, 1966 (softbound).

2. Poems (all signed by "P. O'R." or "Patricia O'Rane")
"My House." *Triad* 6 (June 10, 1921), 27.
"Memory." Ibid. (Aug. 10, 1921), 8.
"Laughter." *Bulletin* (Sydney), July 19, 1923, p. 7.
"Spoil of Dreams." Ibid., Nov. 15, 1923, p. 7.
"Sonnet." Ibid., Dec. 20, 1923, p. 7.
"Imprisoned." Ibid., Feb. 7, 1924, p. 7.
"Inconstant." Ibid., May 8, 1924, p. 7.
"Remorse." Ibid., July 3, 1924, p. 7.
"Vulnerable." Ibid., July 31, 1924, p. 7.
"Two Sonnets." Ibid., Oct. 16, 1924, p. 7.
"Song Makers." Ibid., Dec. 13, 1924, p. 40.
"A Puzzle." *Woman's Mirror* 1 (Feb. 10, 1925), 14.
"My Palette" (three sonnets). *Bulletin*, Feb. 5, 1925, p. 47.
"Sonnet." Ibid., Sept. 10, 1925, p. 7.
"Fugitive." *Woman's Mirror* 2 (Aug. 17, 1926), 14.
"Respite." Ibid. 3 (Jan. 25, 1927), 14.
"Red." *Bulletin*, Feb. 17, 1927, p. 7.
"Two Sonnets." *Muse's Magazine*, Jan., 1929.
"To a Believer." *Stead's Review*, May 1, 1930.
"Song." *Woman's Mirror* 6 (Oct. 14, 1930), 24.
"Lament for a Troubadour." Ibid., 7 (Feb. 3, 1931).
"The Brocaded Curtain." *Bulletin*, Feb. 24, 1932, p. 34.
"Gold." *Woman's Mirror* 9 (April 4, 1933), 14.

3. Short Stories
"Take Your Choice." *Bulletin*, June 7, 1923, pp. 47 - 48, by "Patricia O'Rane."
"The Desire of the Moth." *Art in Australia*, 3rd series, no. 10 (Dec., 1924), n.p., by "Henry Head."

"The Book, the Bishop, and the Ban." *Bulletin*, July 2, 1925, pp. 47 - 48, by "Patricia O'Rane."

"Wheels." Ibid., Dec. 12, 1925, p. 44, by "Patricia O'Rane."

"Wind." Ibid., Jan. 21, 1926, p. 47, by "Patricia O'Rane."

"How Uncle Aubrey Went to London." Ibid., May 30, 1928, p. 57, by "Patricia O'Rane."

"Impulse." Ibid., Jan. 21, 1931, p. 38, by "Patricia O'Rane."

" 'Aunt Nan.' " *Ink* 1 (1932), 43 - 44, by "Patricia O'Rane."

"Hear My Prayer." *Bulletin*, May 2, 1934, pp. 39 - 41, by Eleanor Dark.

"Murder on the Ninth Green." Ibid., Dec. 12, 1934, pp. 28 - 30, by Eleanor Dark.

"The Curtain." *Australian Mercury* 1 (July, 1935), 67 - 75, by Eleanor Dark.

"The Urgent Call." *Home* 16 (Aug. 1, 1935), 44 - 45, by Eleanor Dark.

"Publicity." Ibid. 18 (April 1, 1937), 40+, by Eleanor Dark.

"Water in Moko Creek." *Australia* 2 (March, 1946), 17 - 21, by Eleanor Dark.

4. Articles

"Caroline Chisholm and Her Times." In *The Peaceful Army: A Memorial to the Pioneer Women of Australia*, ed. Flora Eldershaw, pp. 59 - 84. Sydney: Women's Executive Committee and Advisory Council of Australia's 150th Anniversary Celebrations, 1938.

"Australia and the Australians." In *Australia Week-end Book #3*, ed. Sydney Ure Smith and Gwen Morton Spencer, pp. 9 - 19. Sydney: Ure Smith, 1944.

"Drawing a Line Around It." *Writer* (U.S.) 59 (Oct., 1946), 323 - 25.

"They All Come Back." *Walkabout* 17 (Jan. 1, 1951), 19 - 20.

"The Blackall Range Country." Ibid., 21 (Nov. 1, 1955), 18 - 120.

5. Anthologies

Fry, E. M., ed. *Tales by Australians*. London: British Authors' Press, 1939, "Hear My Prayer," pp. 46 - 59.

Roderick, Colin, ed. *The Australian Novel: a Historical Anthology*. Sydney: W. Brooks & Co. [1944 - 45], pp. 287 - 99, from *Sun Across the Sky*.

Chisholm, Alec H. ed. *Land of Wonder: The Best Australian Nature Writing*. Sydney: Angus & Robertson, 1964, pp. 187 - 89, "Introducing Nelson," from *Lantana Lane*.

Ewers, John K. ed. *Modern Australian Short Stories*. Melbourne: Georgian House, 1965, pp. 12 - 24, "The Narrow Escape of Herbie Bassett," from *Lantana Lane*.

6. Unpublished Sources

"What Makes a Good Novel?" symposium broadcast from Radio 2BL, Sydney, March 19, 1951.

Correspondence between Eleanor Dark and A. Grove Day since 1955.

SECONDARY SOURCES

1. Criticism: General

"G.M.M." [George Mackaness?] "A Novelist at Home." *Morning Herald* (Sydney), May 23, 1935, Women's Supplement, p. 17.

ELDERSHAW, M. BARNARD. "Australian Writers, 4: Eleanor Dark." *Bulletin* (Sydney), Nov. 17, 1937, p. 50. A fair summary of achievements before publication of the historical trilogy.

———. *Essays in Australian Fiction.* Melbourne: Melbourne University Press, 1938, pp. 182 - 98. An expanded study of earlier achievements.

ANCHEN, J. O. *The Australian Novel: a Critical Survey.* Melbourne and Sydney: Whitcombe & Tombs, n.d., p. 32. An early survey for school use.

GRATTAN, C. HARTLEY. "Eleanor Dark." In Book-of-the-Month Club *News,* Sept., 1941, p. 2. An excellent early brief biographical note for an American book society.

DEVANNY, JEAN. *Bird of Paradise.* Sydney: Frank Johnson, 1945, pp. 246 - 56, "Writers at Home: Eleanor and Eric Dark." Interview by a personal friend.

LOWE, ERIC. "Novelist with World Audience." *Book News* 1 (Sept., 1946), 79, 81. Comments by another friend.

McKELLAR, JOHN. "The Black and the White." *Southerly* 9, no. 2 (1948), 92 - 98. Historical aspects of *The Timeless Land.*

HEDDLE, ENID MOODIE. *Australian Literature Now.* Melbourne: Longmans, Green, 1949, pp. 51 - 52. Survey, mainly for school use.

KIDDLE, MARGARET. "The Novels of Eleanor Dark." *Week End Review* 1 (Nov. 17, 1950), 259, 261.

RODERICK, COLIN. *Introduction to Australian Fiction.* Sydney: Angus & Robertson, 1950, pp. 140 - 44. Good treatment in a general survey.

BARTLETT, NORMAN. "Letter from Australia." *Christian Science Monitor,* Feb. 9, 1950, p. 15.

LOWE, ERIC. "Eleanor Dark." *Walkabout* 13 (May 1, 1951), 8. Brief description of life and personality by a close friend.

WILKES, G. A. "The Progress of Eleanor Dark." *Southerly,* no. 3 (1951), pp. 139 - 48. Essay by a professor of Australian literature.

LOWE, ERIC. "The Novels of Eleanor Dark." *Meanjin* 10, no. 4 (1951), 341 - 48. Further comment by a friend and fellow novelist.

McKELLAR, JOHN. "Two Australian Novelists' Interpretations of Early History." *Victorian Historical Magazine* 26 (Dec., 1954), 57 - 80. Appreciative remarks on accuracy of portrayal of historical figures in the trilogy and in Ernestine Hill's *My Love Must Wait.*

MILLER, E. MORRIS and MACARTNEY, FREDERICK T. *Australian Literature.* Sydney: Angus & Robertson, 1956, pp. 136 - 38. Commentary in a general survey.

MANIFOLD, JOHN. "Our Writers, VIII: Eleanor Dark." *Overland*, no. 15 (July, 1959), p. 39. Sketch by a fiction writer and poet who terms the historical trilogy "the nearest thing we have to a national epic."

HADGRAFT, CECIL. *Australian Literature: A Critical Account*. London: Heinemann, 1960. A brief standard critical volume by an English professor.

GREEN, H. M. *A History of Australian Literature*. 2 vols. Sydney: Angus & Robertson, 1961, passim. The most extensive historical survey by a profound scholar.

HADGRAFT, CECIL. "Literature." In *The Pattern of Australian Culture*, p. 87. Ithaca, N.Y.: Cornell University Press, 1963.

HESELTINE, H. P. "The Modern Australian Novel." *The Teaching of English* (Journal of the English Teachers' Association of New South Wales), no. 3 (1963), pp. 35 - 37.

KEESING, NANCY. "Review." *Bulletin*, Aug. 24, 1963, p. 42.

MURRAY-SMITH, STEPHEN. "Darkness at Dawn." *Australian Book Review* 2 (Sept., 1963), 178. Lengthy review of reprinted edition of historical trilogy.

HESELTINE, H. P. "Australian Fiction Since 1920." In *The Literature of Australia*, ed. Geoffrey Dutton, pp. 198 - 99, 205 - 6, 222. Adelaide: Penguin Books, 1964. Part of an excellent brief survey.

EWERS, JOHN K. *Creative Writing in Australia*, 5th rev. ed. Melbourne: Georgian House, 1966, pp. 36, 80 - 82.

BLAKE, L. J. *Australian Writers*. Adelaide: Rigby, 1968, pp. 150 - 51.

MOORE, T. INGLIS. *Social Patterns in Australian Literature*. Sydney: Angus & Robertson, 1971, passim. Occasional references in connection with social aspects of the author's works.

McQUEEN, HUMPHREY. "The Novels of Eleanor Dark." *Hemisphere* (Canberra) 17 (Jan., 1973), 38 - 41. A recent reappraisal.

SERLE, GEOFFREY. *From Deserts the Prophets Come: The Creative Spirit in Australia, 1788 - 1972*. Melbourne: Heinemann, 1973.

2. Criticism: Specific Full Reviews

*Prelude to Christopher*
"Prelude to Christopher." *Herald* (Melbourne), May 19, 1934.

"Prelude to Christopher." *Daily Telegraph* (Sydney), May 19, 1934.

"A Modern Ophelia." *Morning Herald* (Sydney), May 25, 1934. p. 5.

"Prelude to Christopher." *Bulletin*, May 30, 1934. p. 5.

PALMER, NETTIE. "Prelude to Christopher." *All About Books* 7 (June 12, 1934), 115.

SPRING, HOWARD. "A Eugenic Tragedy." *Evening Standard* (London), Nov. 5, 1936.

## Return to Coolami

"Across the Blue Mountains." *Times* (London) *Literary Supplement*, Feb. 1, 1936, p. 92.

"An Australian Story." *Morning Herald*, Feb. 21, 1936, p. 7.

MACARTNEY, F. T. "Two Good Novels." *All About Books* 8 (April 11, 1936), 53.

"R.P." "Several Novels by Women." *Bulletin*, April 22, 1936, pp. 2 - 4.

DICKSON, S. "Discovery of Contentment in Australia." *New York Herald-Tribune* (New York), June 14, 1936, p. 8.

HUNTER, R. "Sorrows of Susan." *Sun* (New York), June 13, 1936.

KAZIN, ALFRED. "Australian Journey." *New York Times Book Review*, June 14, 1936, p. 16.

"A.C." "Fiction." *Saturday Review of Literature* (New York) 14 (June 20, 1936), 19.

SPRING, HOWARD. "Return to Coolami." *Evening Standard* (London), Nov. 5, 1936.

## Sun Across the Sky

"An Australian Day." *Times* (London) *Literary Supplement*, Aug. 7, 1937, p. 575.

"Eleanor Dark's New Novel." *Bulletin*, Sept. 22, 1937, p. 8.

"Novels of the Day." *Morning Herald*, Sept. 24, 1937, p. 7.

"Eleanor Dark's Novels." *All About Books* 9 (Oct. 12, 1937), 150.

"All in a Day." *Morning Herald* (supplement), Oct. 26, 1937, p. 2.

PRUETTE, L. "Sun Across the Sky." *New York Herald-Tribune*, Oct. 31, 1937, pp. 10, 14.

FIELD, L. "A Pair of Geniuses." *New York Times Book Review*, Nov. 14, 1937.

## Waterway

"Novels of the Day: A Sydney Day." *Morning Herald*, June 24, 1938, p. 6.

HUTCHINSON, P. "A Dramatic Novel of Australia." *New York Times Book Review*, Aug. 7, 1938, p. 6.

DANGERFIELD, G. "Twenty-four Hours in the Antipodes." *Saturday Review of Literature* 18 (Aug. 13, 1938), 6.

HARROP, M. "Waterway." *New York Herald-Tribune*, Aug. 14, 1938, pp. 7 - 8.

"Love and Tragedy on Sydney Harbour." *Sun* (Sydney), Feb. 2, 1947. Later reviews cover the 1946 reprint.

"A Local Novel Comes Home." *Daily Telegraph*, Feb. 22, 1947.

"Art and Accident." *Bulletin*, March 5, 1947, p. 2.

## The Timeless Land

DAVIS, HASSOLDT. "Out of Australia." *Nation* (New York) 153 (Oct. 4, 1941), 316.

Lambrecht, Klaus. "It Happened in Australia." *Saturday Review of Literature* 24 (Oct. 4, 1941), 5.

Rugoff, Milton. "Birth of a Nation — Down in Australia." *Herald-Tribune*, Oct. 5, 1941, p. 5.

Woods, Katherine. "Eleanor Dark's Novel of Australia's Settlement." *New York Times Book Review*, Oct. 5, 1941, pp. 5, 18.

Thompson, Ralph. "The Timeless Land." *New York Times*, Oct. 8, 1941, p. 21.

"T.L." "The Timeless Land." *Age* (Melbourne), Nov. 1, 1941.

"Novels of the Week: Redemption." *Times Literary Supplement*, Nov. 1, 1941, p. 541. "First choice."

"Terra Incognita." *Morning Herald*, Dec. 20, 1941, p. 8.

"Two Historical Novels." *Bulletin*, Jan. 7, 1942, p. 2.

Barker, Uther. "Matrix of the Past." *B.P. Magazine*, June 1, 1942, pp. 62 - 63.

"Looking Backward." *Manas* (Los Angeles) 5 (May 7, 1952), 3 - 4.

Thomson, Andrew K. *Understanding the Novel: The Timeless Land.* Brisbane: Jacaranda Press, 1966.


*The Little Company*

"Man and Sociology." *Bulletin*, July 11, 1945, 2.

"The Little Company." *Australia's Progress* 1 (Aug. 24, 1945), 15.

"Miss Bronte." "Torture, Step by Step." *Telegraph*, (Sydney), July 14, 1945, p. 13.

Barker, Uther. "The Little Company." *Meanjin Papers*, no. 2 (1946), p. 167.

Baer, Howard. "The Little Company." *News* (Chicago), June 13, 1945.

Frederick, John T. "I've Been Reading." *Sun* (Chicago), May 13, 1945.

Martin, Jane. "The Little Company." *New York Times Books*, May 20, 1945, pp. 16 - 17.

Prescott, Orville. "The Little Company." *New York Times*, May 9, 1945, p. 21.

Sapieha, Virginia. "The Little Company." *New York Herald-Tribune*, May 13, 1945, p. 6.

Russell, Archer. "The Little Company." *Australia's Progress*, Aug. 24, 1945, p. 15.

Maes, Nuri. "The Little Company." *Australian Women's Digest*, Dec., 1945, pp. 14 - 15.


*Storm of Time*

"L.V.K." "New Fiction." *Morning Herald*, Oct. 30, 1948, p. 6.

"Storm of Time." *Times* (London) *Literary Supplement*, July 15, 1949, p. 457.

Cubis, Dorothy. "Storm of Time." *Journal*, Royal Australian Historical Society, 35 (1949), 65 - 68.

BARKER, UTHER. "Storm of Time." *Southerly,* no. 2 (1950), pp. 101 - 103.

RUGG, WINNIFRED KEAN. "Phrased with Grave Beauty." *Christian Science Monitor,* Feb. 9, 1950, p. 15.

BURGER, NASH K. "Old Australia." *New York Times Book Review,* Feb. 5, 1950, p. 30.

DAVIS ELRICK B. "When Bligh of the *Bounty* Ruled Australia." *New York Herald-Tribune,* Jan. 29, 1950, p. 5.

HAAS, VICTOR P. "Bligh of Botany Bay." *Saturday Review of Literature* 30 (Feb. 25, 1950), 19.

TORKELSON, LUCILE. "Storm of Time." *Journal* (Milwaukee), March 5, 1950.

*No Barrier*

"When Macquarie Ruled." *Age* (Melbourne), June 20, 1953.

"*No Barrier* Falls Short." *Daily Mail,* June 28, 1953, p. 17.

BAKER, SIDNEY. "The Great Australian Novel?" *Morning Herald,* July 11, 1953, p. 8. Considers the trilogy as a completed saga.

TONKIN, MURRAY. "Beyond the Mountains a New Land." *News* (Adelaide), July 12, 1953.

"Three Australian Novels. " *Bulletin,* July 15, 1953, p. 2. Considers the completed trilogy.

KEESING, NANCY. "No Barrier." *Bulletin,* Aug. 24, 1953, p. 42.

SHAW, A. G. L. "No Barrier." *Meanjin* 12 no. 3 (1953), 342 - 43.

"A Very Human Villain." *A.M.* (Sydney), Feb. 16, 1954.

*Lantana Lane*

"Salt of the Earth." *Times Literary Supplement,* April 10, 1959.

MAIR, IAN. "Pineapples Among the Lantana." *Age* (Melbourne), May 6, 1959.

COVELL, ROGER. "Eleanor Dark Turns Out a Good One." *Courier-Mail* (Brisbane), May 9, 1959.

"Pineapple Soufflé." *British Weekly* (London), May 14, 1959.

BAKER, SIDNEY. "Our Good Earth." *Morning Herald,* May 23, 1959, p. 13.

"About Farmers: And Lantana." *Canberra Times,* May 30, 1959.

"There's Nothing — and Nobody — Dull in Lantana Lane." *Mercury* (Melbourne), June 11, 1959.

"Happy Families." *Bulletin,* June 24, 1959, p. 2.

HENRY, R. "Lantana Lane." *Books and Bookmen* 4 (June, 1959), 15.

"A Community in Queensland." *Press* (Christchurch, N.Z.), Aug. 8, 1959.

3. Other Sources

*Australian Encyclopedia,* 5th ed. Sydney: Grolier Society, 1965.

CLARK, MANNING. *A Short History of Australia.* New York: New American Library, 1963.

COBLEY, DR. JOHN, ed. *Sydney Cove, 1788: The First Year of Settlement in Australia.* London: Hodder & Stoughton, 1962.

————. *Sydney Cove, 1789 - 90.* Sydney: Angus & Robertson, 1963.

————. *Sydney Cove, 1791 - 92.* Sydney: Angus & Robertson, 1965.

DARK, ERIC P. *Medicine and the Social Order.* Sydney: Printed for the author, [1942].

————. *Who are the Reds.* Sydney: Printed for the author, 1946. Foreword by Eleanor Dark.

————. *The World Against Russia.* Sydney: Pinchgut Press, 1948.

————. *The Press Against the People.* Sydney: Published by the author [1949].

ELLIS, MALCOLM H. *Lachlan Macquarie.* Sydney: Dymock, 1947.

————. *John Macarthur.* Sydney: Angus & Robertson, 1955.

HORNE, DONALD. *The Next Australia.* Sydney: Angus & Robertson, 1971.

JONES, JOSEPH and JOHANNA. *Authors and Areas of Australia.* Austin, Texas: Steck, Vaughn Co., 1970, pp. 16 - 17.

MACKANESS, GEORGE. *Admiral Arthur Phillip.* Sydney: Angus & Robertson, 1937.

————. *The Life of Vice-Admiral William Bligh, R.N., F.R.S.* Sydney: Angus & Robertson, 1951; rev. ed. 1956.

O'REILLY, M(OLLIE). *Dowell O'Reilly from His Letters.* London: Simpkin, Marshall, Hamilton, Kent & Co., 1927.

*The Prose and Verse of Dowell O'Reilly*, with preface by D.G.F. Sydney: Angus & Robertson, 1924.

RAWSON, GEOFFREY. *Bligh of the "Bounty."* London: P. Allen & Co., 1930; rev. ed. 1934.

*Who's Who in Australia.* Melbourne: Herald, 1971.

# Index

(The works of Mrs. Dark are listed under her name. Fictional characters or places are not indexed.)